Opus 69

Rathaus Bremen

**Text
Georg Skalecki**

**Photographien / Photographs
Christian Richters**

Edition Axel Menges

Herausgeber/Editor: Axel Menges

© 2009 Edition Axel Menges, Stuttgart / London
ISBN 978-3-932565-69-4

Alle Rechte vorbehalten, besonders die der Übersetzung in andere Sprachen.
All rights reserved, especially those of translation into other languages.

Druck/Printing: Druckhaus Waiblingen, Waiblingen
Bindearbeiten/Binding: Buchbinderei Karl Dieringer GmbH, Gerlingen

Übersetzung ins Englische/Translation into English: Michael Robinson
Lektorat/Editing: Dorothea Duwe
Design: Axel Menges

Inhalt

6 Georg Skalecki: Das Rathaus in Bremen
Zur Geschichte der Freien Hansestadt Bremen 6 – Die Form der Stadt 8 – Baugeschichte des Rathauses 10 – Zur Bautypologie 14 – Ikonographie 18 – Der Roland 18 – Das Neue Rathaus 20 – Das Rathaus heute 20 – Literaturauswahl 20

22 Historische Photographie und Grundrisse

24 Bildteil
Außenaufnahmen 24 – Untere Halle im Alten Rathaus 42 – Obere Halle im Alten Rathaus 44 – Güldenkammer 50 – Untere Halle im Neuen Rathaus 52 – Obere Halle im Neuen Rathaus 54 – Senatssaal 58 – Festsaal 60 – Kaiserkabinett 63 – Kaminzimmer 64 – Gobelinzimmer 66 – Bibliothekszimmer 67 – Hauptraum im Ratskeller 68 – Hauffkeller 69 – Bacchuskeller 69 – Kaiserzimmer 70 – Rosekeller 71

72 Danksagung

Contents

7 Georg Skalecki: The town hall in Bremen
About the history of the Free Hanseatic City of Bremen 7 – The form of the city 9 – The building history of the town hall 11 – About the typology of the building 15 – Iconography 19 – The Roland 19 – The new town hall 21 – The town hall today 21 – Selected bibliography 21

22 Historical photograph and floor plans

24 Pictorial section
Exterior views 24 – Lower hall in the old town hall 42 – Upper hall in the old town hall 44 – Güldenkammer 50 – Lower hall in the new town hall 52 – Upper hall in the new town hall 54 – Senate hall 58 – Banqueting hall 60 – Kaiserkabinett 63 – Fireplace room 64 – Gobelin room 66 – Library room 67 – Main room in the Ratskeller 68 – Hauffkeller 69 – Bacchuskeller 69 – Kaiserzimmer 70 – Rosekeller 71

72 Word of thanks

Georg Skalecki
Das Rathaus in Bremen

Das Rathaus und die dazugehörige Roland-Statue auf dem Marktplatz in Bremen zählen zum Weltkulturerbe der UNESCO. Im Jahr 2004 erfolgte die Aufnahme in diese Liste der herausragenden Zeugnisse der Architektur- und Kulturgeschichte, also exakt zum 600. Geburtstag der Roland-Statue.

1404 begann ein umfangreiches architektonisches und städtebauliches Selbstdarstellungsprojekt der nach Unabhängigkeit strebenden Hansestadt Bremen mit der Aufstellung einer »Freiheitsstatue« und der Planung eines repräsentativen Rathauses, mit dem im darauffolgenden Jahr begonnen wurde. Dieser gotische Rathausbau verkörpert das Idealbild des für die europäisch-abendländische Geschichte mit ihren republikanischen städtischen Gemeinwesen so wichtigen Bautypus. Aufgrund seines hohen Grades an Authentizität und seiner ungestörten Überlieferung – und auch wegen der bedauerlichen Verluste anderer typischer Rathausgroßbauten vergleichbarer europäischer Stadtrepubliken – ist das Bremer Rathaus der beste und typischste Repräsentant dieser Bauaufgabe. Es zeigt lehrbuchartig die Grundform der mittelalterlichen und frühneuzeitlichen Rathausbautypologie. Das Bremer Rathaus hat – vielleicht aufgrund seiner weitsichtigen Erstkonzeption – später keine wesentlichen Veränderungen erfahren. Einzig zwischen 1595 und 1616 ist das Bauwerk vorsichtig fortgeschrieben worden, indem es ein erweitertes Fassadenbildprogramm in den aktuellen Formen der Weserrenaissance erhielt. Damit wurde der Anspruch auf Reichsfreiheit der Stadt erneut unterstrichen und ergänzt durch eine geradezu enzyklopädische bildliche Ausstattung, an der exemplarisch der hohe humanistische Bildungsanspruch der Zeit in Form der Ikonographie mit seinen weitreichenden politischen und religiösen allegorischen Themen dargestellt wird. Das Alte Rathaus blieb danach architektonisch unangetastet, auch noch als Ende des 19. Jahrhunderts die Aufgaben der städtischen Verwaltung zunahmen und zusätzliche Räume erforderten. Dieser Bedarf wurde durch einen rückwärtig angesetzten Erweiterungsbau gedeckt, den der Münchener Architekt Gabriel von Seidl dem bestehenden Bau feinfühlig unterordnete, ohne dass er auf architektonische Qualität seiner Neuschöpfung verzichtete. Mit Weitsicht entschieden sich die Ratsherren damals für eine gekonnte Fortschreibung des Bestehenden, ohne dieses anzutasten oder durch den Erweiterungsbau zu bedrängen. Deshalb ist neben dem Alten Rathaus auch dessen Erweiterung als eine höchst gelungene Leistung in städtebaulicher und baukünstlerischer Hinsicht zu werten.

Für die besondere Bedeutung des Bremer Rathauses im Sinne der UNESCO spricht, dass es sich um ein architektonisch außergewöhnliches spätmittelalterliches Bauensemble handelt. Es steht gleichzeitig symbolhaft für die republikanisch-kommunalen Verwaltungsstrukturen der europäischen politischen Geschichte. Die Freie Hansestadt Bremen ist die älteste europäische Stadtrepublik, die – jetzt in der Form eines deutschen Bundeslandes – in gewisser Hinsicht ihre Selbstständigkeit bis heute bewahrt hat. Ohne Zweifel stellt das Bremer Rathaus den Idealtyp für die kulturhistorisch bedeutsame Bauaufgabe »Rathaus« dar. Mit seiner architektonischen Form des querrechteckigen Saalgeschossbaus, der sich traufseitig und mit Arkadengang zum Marktplatz hin ausrichtet, und mit seinem für spätmittelalterlich-repräsentative Rathausbauten charakteristischen Bildprogramm, das den Anspruch städtischer Ratsherrschaft zeigt, ragt das Bremer Rathaus aus den noch bestehenden Bauten dieser Art heraus. Am Bauwerk selbst kann die 600jährige Geschichte der autonomen Staatsverfassung abgelesen werden. Das hier nachvollziehbare freiheitsverbundene Prinzip der Republik ist wichtiger Bestandteil der Geschichte der europäischen Städte.

Zur Geschichte der Freien Hansestadt Bremen

Die besondere topographische Situation einer mehrere Kilometer langen und bis 11 m über dem Meeresspiegel hohen Düne parallel zur Weser, die mit ihren Enden an die eiszeitlichen Geesterhebungen anschließt, war als hochwassersicherer Handelsweg und Ansiedlungspunkt bestens geeignet. So belegen Bodenfunde von der vorrömischen Eisenzeit bis hin zur karolingischen Zeit eine kontinuierliche vor- und frühgeschichtliche menschliche Nutzung dieses Bereiches. In eine schon bestehende kleine Siedlung hinein wurde auf Weisung des späteren Kaisers Karls des Großen im Jahr 787 vom angelsächsischen Missionar Willehad eine erste Domkirche erbaut, deren Weihe 789 erfolgte. Willehad war der erste Bischof, und er sollte von Bremen aus die Christianisierung der nördlichen Teile des Frankenreiches betreiben. Rund 50 Jahre nach der Gründung des Bistums Bremen – wohl um 834 – folgte Hamburg als weiteres Bistum des Nordens, das aber schon bald nach dem Überfall durch die Wikinger 845 wieder aufgegeben wurde. Bremen blieb danach zunächst wichtigstes Zentrum und wurde zum Erzbistum erhoben, dessen erster Erzbischof Ansgar war. Aufgrund dieser einzigartigen Stellung Bremens erfolgte von hier aus dann die Christianisierung des gesamten europäischen Nordens, so dass die Stadt die Rolle eines »Roms des Nordens« einnahm. Island, Grönland (die amerikanische Küste soll sogar erreicht worden sein), Norwegen, Schweden und das Baltikum wurden von Bremen aus missioniert und Bistümer gegründet. So waren zum Beispiel Lund und Riga bremische Gründungen, die bis zu ihrer Erhebung als eigene Erzbistümer der Bremer Kirchenprovinz unterstellt blieben. Den Chronisten des Bremer Doms ist durch ihre frühen Berichte zu verdanken, dass sich das Wissen über die Verhältnisse des europäischen Nordens über die Grenzen des damaligen abendländischen Kulturkreises hinaus erweiterte. Die Schriften des Domkanonikers Adam von Bremen (1072–81) sind wichtige Dokumente mittelalterlicher Historiographie.

Diese herausragende Stellung fand auch ihren Niederschlag in der architektonischen und städtebaulichen Entwicklung. Nach dem Gründungsbau der Domkirche, der noch in Holz oder Fachwerk ausgeführt war, entstand nach 805 der erste Dom in Stein, dem nach einem Brand 1041 ein Neubau nach dem Vorbild rheinischer frühmittelalterlicher Großbauten, besonders wohl des karolingischen Kölner Doms, folgte. Von diesem Bau des 11. Jahrhunderts haben sich im heutigen Dom erhebliche Teile erhalten, die mit ihren Ausmaßen sowie ihrer architektonischen und künstlerischen Qualität die damalige Bedeutung Bremens erahnen lassen.

Neben dem Dom und der später auch ummauerten Domimmunität entwickelten sich zeitgleich ein Markt und eine Kaufmannssiedlung. Am 5. Juni 888 wurde

Georg Skalecki
The town hall in Bremen

The town hall and the statue of Roland associated with it in Bremen's market place enjoy UNESCO World Heritage status. They joined this list of outstanding examples of architectural and cultural history in the year 2004, in other words exactly on the 600th anniversary of the statue of Roland.

1404 saw the beginning of an extensive architectural and urban development self-promotion project by the Hanseatic City of Bremen, which was striving for independence. It set up a »statue of liberty« and planned an imposing town hall on which work started in the following year. This Gothic town hall is an ideal image of this building type that is so important for European and Western history with its republican urban community life. Because of its high degree of authenticity and its unbroken tradition – and also because of the regrettable loss of other large town halls in comparable European city republics – Bremen town hall is the best and most typical representative of this building task. It is a text-book example of the basic form of medieval and early modern town hall typology. Bremen town hall – perhaps because the initial concept was so far-sighted – has never changed significantly. All that has happened was that building was carefully continued between 1595 and 1616: it acquired an extended façade image programme in the forms of the Weser Renaissance that was under way at the time. This one more underlined the city's claim to immediacy as a free imperial city. The figurative decoration is almost encyclopaedic in its scope, showing the period's striving for humanistic education in the form of iconography with a wide-ranging political and religious spectrum of allegorical themes. The old town hall remained untouched architecturally after this, even in the late 19th century, when the city administration had acquired greater responsibilities, and thus needed more space. An extension was finally added at the back of the building, which Munich architect Gabriel von Seidl sensitively subordinated to the existing structure, without detracting from the architectural quality of his own building. The councillors were far-sighted enough at that time to opt for a skilful continuation of the existing town hall, without touching it or allowing the new building to oppress it. For this reason the new town hall in Bremen is to be assessed as one of the most successful achievements from an urban and artistic point of view.

This is an architecturally extraordinary late medieval building ensemble, which further emphasizes Bremen town hall's special significance in the spirit of UNESCO. At the same time, it symbolizes European history's republican administration structures based on local politics. The Free Hanseatic City of Bremen is the oldest city republic in Europe, and to a certain extent – now in the form of a German *Land* in its own right – it has retained its independence to the present day in a certain respect. There is no doubt that Bremen town hall represents the ideal type for this culturally important building brief, the »town hall«. With its architectural form as a rectangular hall building with several storeys, with its eaves and an arcade facing the market place, and with the usual pictorial programme for a prestigious late medieval town hall building, showing the status of the municipal councillors, Bremen town hall is outstanding among the surviving buildings of this kind. It is possible to read the 600-year history of the autonomous state constitution from the building itself. The principle of the republic, with freedom as its guideline, can be clearly understood here, and that is an important component of the history of European cities.

About the history of the Free Hanseatic City of Bremen

The particular topographical situation of a dune several kilometres long and up to 11 m above sea level parallel with the Weser, its ends connecting up with the ice-age eminences of the geest, was entirely suitable as a trade route that was safe from floods and as a settlement site. Archaeological finds from the pre-Roman iron age to the Carolingian era prove continuous prehistoric and early settlement on this site. The Anglo-Saxon missionary Willehad built a first cathedral church on this site in a small existing settlement, on instructions from the later emperor Charlemagne in 787. The church was consecrated in 789. Willehad was the first bishop, and he was intended to convert the northern part of the Frankish empire to Christianity from Bremen. About 50 years after the bishopric of Bremen was established – probably about 834 – Hamburg followed as the second northern bishopric, but this was abandoned shortly after raids by the Vikings in 845. Bremen remained the most important centre after this, and was raised to an archbishopric, with Ansgar as the first archbishop. The whole of the European north was then indeed converted from here as a result of Bremen's unique position, so the city took on the role of a »Rome of the North«. Missionaries from Bremen went out to Iceland, Greenland (it is even said that the coast of North America was reached), Norway, Sweden and the Baltic, and bishoprics were established. Lund and Riga were founded by Bremen, for example, and they remained subject to the Bremen ecclesiastical province until they were raised to the status of bishoprics in their own right. We have the Bremen cathedral chroniclers to thank for the fact that their early reports spread knowledge about circumstances in the European north beyond the boundaries of what was then the Western cultural sphere. The writings of cathedral canon Adam von Bremen (1072–81) are important documents of medieval historiography.

This outstanding position also affected architectural and urban development. After the foundation building for the cathedral church, which was in wood or a timber frame, the first stone cathedral was built after 805, and this was followed after a fire in 1041 by a new building modelled on large early medieval structures in the Rhineland, and probably the Carolingian Cologne cathedral in particular. Considerable parts of this 11th century building have survived in the present cathedral. Its dimensions and its architectural and artistic quality give a sense of how important Bremen was at the time.

A market and a merchants' settlement developed at the same time as the cathedral and the cathedral immunity, which was later walled. Bremen was granted market, mint and customs rights on 5 June 888, and this was confirmed in 965 by Emperor Otto I. This meant that special incomes flowed into the archdiocese, and the merchants were afforded royal protec-

Bremen das Markt-, Münz- und Zollrecht erteilt, das 965 von Kaiser Otto I. bestätigt wurde, womit dem Erzstift besondere Einkünfte zuflossen und den Kaufleuten königlicher Schutz zugesprochen wurde. Damit wird deutlich, dass Bremen schon im 9. Jahrhundert auch ein namhafter Handelsstandort gewesen sein muss. Unterhalb des Doms bis hin zur Balge, einem Nebenarm der Weser, entwickelte sich ein Marktplatz mit Schiffsanlegestelle und damit auch allmählich eine innere Stadtstruktur. Bedeutende archäologische Funde, so ein Schiff von 805, belegen eine aktive Handelstätigkeit im Frühmittelalter. Die Markt- und Kaufmannskirche St. Veit, später Unser Lieben Frauen, bestand mindestens seit dem 10. Jahrhundert und trug ebenfalls zur Entwicklung des stadträumlichen Bereichs bei.

Im 12. und 13. Jahrhundert entwickelte sich eine bürgerliche Selbstverwaltung, die 1186 von Kaiser Friedrich Barbarossa in ihren Rechten bestätigt wurde. 1225 – außergewöhnlich früh für den deutschsprachigen Raum – war die erste Nennung von politisch handelnden Ratsherren, die sich selbst – ähnlich wie in italienischen Stadtrepubliken – als »Consules« bezeichneten. Die Stadt selbst hatte zu dieser Zeit eine Größe von etwa 10 000 Einwohnern erreicht. Die Stellung des Erzbischofs verlor zunehmend an Bedeutung, während sich eine konkrete Stadtverfassung herausbildete. 1303/04 wurde ein auf dem Gewohnheitsrecht basierendes Stadtrecht im Auftrag des Rates niedergeschrieben. Damit festigte sich kontinuierlich die städtische Regierung, deren Privilegien selbstbewusst eingefordert wurden. Der Erzbischof wurde aus der Stadt gedrängt und nahm Zuflucht in seiner Burg in Bremervörde. In dieser Zeit des gewachsenen Selbstbewusstseins dank wirtschaftlicher und politischer Erstarkung erfolgte als symbolhafter Akt die Aufstellung des Rolands, der als Sendbote Kaiser Karls des Großen schon bei der legendären Stadtgründung die Freiheitsrechte überbracht haben soll. Auch der Neubau eines sehr großen Rathauses ist als politisch-demonstratives Zeichen zu werten. Die gewonnene Selbstständigkeit und Unabhängigkeit wurden zunächst erfolgreich ohne formelle Bestätigung verteidigt, bis schließlich die Stadt auch die offizielle Anerkennung ihrer Freiheit erhielt. Am 1. Juni 1646 verlieh Kaiser Ferdinand III. im »Linzer Diplom« der Hansestadt Bremen die Rechte einer unmittelbaren freien Reichsstadt.

Die weitreichenden Handelsbeziehungen der Stadt entwickelten sich vollkommen autark, und die Stadt entzog sich sogar dem damals weitreichenden Einfluss der Hanse. Erst 1358 trat Bremen der Hanse bei, um die Handelskonflikte geschickt zum eigenen Nutzen regeln zu können. Mit Lübeck, Köln und Hamburg wurde Bremen zur wichtigen Kraft innerhalb der Hanse, bis diese Mitte des 17. Jahrhunderts ihre Bedeutung endgültig verlor.

Mit der 1646 erlangten offiziellen Reichsfreiheit blieb Bremen zunächst unabhängig innerhalb Deutschlands und entwickelte sich kontinuierlich weiter. Auch nach der napoleonischen Besetzung erlangte die Stadt auf dem Wiener Kongress 1815 ihre volle Unabhängigkeit als souveräner Staat im Deutschen Bund wieder. Die dann durch die allgemeine Gleichschaltung in der nationalsozialistischen Zeit verlorene Eigenständigkeit gaben nach dem Krieg die Amerikaner der Stadt unter dem bedeutenden Bürgermeister Wilhelm Kaisen zurück; sie beanspruchten 1947 Bremen und Bremerhaven innerhalb des Britischen Sektors als Enklave, um ihren Nachschub über die Häfen zu organisieren. Mit dieser aktuellen Sonderstellung eröffnete sich der Weg zur neuerlichen Selbstständigkeit. 1949 wurde Bremen mit den eingemeindeten Gebieten und der Stadt Bremerhaven ein eigenständiges Bundesland innerhalb der neugegründeten Bundesrepublik Deutschland und setzt damit die Tradition der freien Stadt fort.

Die Form der Stadt

Die Düne als Erhebung über der Weser wurde dank ihrer begünstigten Lage als geeignete Stelle für eine Ansiedlung ausgewählt. Der höchste Punkt der Düne wiederum war für Willehad der beste Standort für seinen Dom. Zu dessen Füßen bis an die Balge heran muss schon früh ein Marktplatz bestanden haben, wenn auch ein älteres Rathaus nicht unmittelbar an diesem Platz, sondern weiter westlich gelegen hat. Mit dem Bau des neuen Rathauses im Jahr 1405 wurde dann auch stadträumlich ein neues, festes Gefüge entwickelt, das bis heute die innere Anlage der Stadt prägt. Es handelt sich um eine Platzraumfolge, deren Mittelpunkt der Marktplatz ist und die als eine Art »Forum« eine zentrale Stellung behielt. Obwohl der Dom mit seiner Westfassade nicht weit entfernt liegt, wurde er durch die geschickte Positionierung des Rathausbaus etwas ins Abseits gedrängt. Den Neubau des Rathauses setzte man in die Achse des alten Fernhandelsweges, so dass von Osten wie von Westen die Straße auf die Schmalseiten des Rathauses und die dortigen großen Portale für die Untere Halle zuläuft. Die südliche Langseite des Rathauses nimmt als geschlossene Platzfront die gesamte Nordseite des Marktplatzes ein, bestimmt ihn somit städtebaulich. Das Rathaus ist damit das alles beherrschende Bauwerk dieses zentralen Platzes. Daran schließen sich – jeweils nach kurzen Verengungen – weitere Platzräume an: nach Nordosten der Domshof, nach Nordwesten der Liebfrauenkirchhof. Die rechte Flanke wird vom alten geistlichen Zentrum, dem Dom, besetzt, die linke Flanke von der Ratskirche Unser Lieben Frauen. Diese Ordnung wurde weiter fortentwickelt, indem 1537/38 als unmittelbares Gegenüber zum Rathaus die Kaufleute den Schütting als Sitz ihrer Interessenvertretung bauten. Die West- und die Ostseite des Marktplatzes wurden mit giebelständigen kleineren Privathäusern bebaut, durchaus repräsentativ, aber als kleinteilig parzellierte Einzelbauten in additiver Reihung, die somit eine untergeordnete Verbindung zwischen den Großbauten herstellten. Mit der Bebauung war ein Rahmen um den Marktplatz gebildet, der die öffentliche Nutzung für entscheidende Ereignisse förderte. Neben dem Marktbetrieb wurden hier Gericht gehalten, Entscheidungen des Rates verkündet, Zeremonien begangen und politische Kundgebungen abgehalten. Der Markt war und ist öffentliches Zentrum mit politischer Bedeutung.

Die Stadt entwickelte sich weiter, erhielt weitere Pfarrkirchen und eine mittelalterliche Ummauerung, die man im 17. Jahrhundert ausbaute und verstärkte. Damit war die Größe der Stadt festgeschrieben. Historische Stadtansichten des 16. und 17. Jahrhunderts zeigen die Situation sehr deutlich. Das Rathaus mit Markt bildete das städtebauliche Zentrum. Um die Pfarrkirchen herum entstanden eigene Quartiere, in denen Bürgerhäuser mit giebelständigen Stellungen das Straßenbild prägten. Die gesamte Stadt wurde von einer Stadtbefestigung umfasst, die man 1802 aufgab und in eine gartenkünstle-

tion. This made it clear that Bremen must have been an important trading post even in the 9th century. A market place with moorings developed below the cathedral towards the Balge, a tributary of the Weser, and with it came an inner urban structure. Important archaeological finds, such as a ship dating from 805, provide evidence of vigorous trading activity in the early middle ages. The market and the merchants' church of St. Veit, later Unser Lieben Frauen, existed from the 10th century at least and also contributed to the development of the urban area.

In the 12th and 13th century an independent bourgeois administration developed, and its rights were confirmed in 1186 by Emperor Frederick Barbarossa. In 1225 – extraordinarily early for the German-speaking world – councillors acting politically were mentioned for the first time. They called themselves »consules«, similarly to the practice in Italian city republics. The city itself had reached the size of about 10,000 inhabitants. The role of the archbishop became increasingly less important, while a concrete city constitution emerged. A city law based on common law was written down at the council's behest in 1303/04. This continually strengthened the city government, which confidently insisted on its privileges. The archbishop was forced out of the city and took refuge in his castle at Bremervörde. The Roland was erected as a symbolic act at this time of mature self-confidence thanks to increased economic and political strength. In the legend of the city's foundation, Roland was said to have handed over the freedom rights, as Charlemagne's messenger. The building of a new and very large town hall is also to be seen as a demonstrative political sign. The autonomy and independence acquired were successfully defended without formal confirmation at first, until finally the city's freedom was formally recognized as well. On 1 June 1646, Emperor Ferdinand III granted the Hanseatic City of Bremen the rights of an immediate and free imperial city in the »Linzer Diplom«.

The city's far-reaching trading connections developed with complete economic self-sufficiency, and the city even eschewed the influence of the Hanseatic League, which was extensive by that time. Bremen did not join the Hanseatic League until 1358, when it skilfully resolved trading conflicts to its own advantage. With Lübeck, Cologne and Hamburg, Bremen became an important force in the League, until this finally lost its significance in the mid 17th century.

After acquiring imperial freedom officially in 1646, Bremen remained independent within Germany first of all, and continued to develop. Even after the Napoleonic occupation, the city regained its complete independence as a sovereign state in the German Federation at the Congress of Vienna in 1815. After general subjection to conformity under the National Socialists, the Americans restored its lost independence to the city under its important mayor Wilhelm Kaisen. The Americans has claimed Bremen and Bremerhaven as an enclave inside the British sector in 1947 so that they could organize supplies and personnel movements via the harbours. This special status at that time opened up the way to modern independence. In 1949, Bremen and its incorporated areas and the town of Bremerhaven became an independent *Land* within the German Federal Republic and thus continues the tradition of the free city.

The form of the city

The dune as an eminence above the Weser was chosen as a suitable place for a settlement thanks to its favourable position. Willehad in his turn chose the highest point on the dune as the best location for his cathedral. There must have been a market place at its feet on the land slowing down to the Balge, though the older town hall was not sited directly on this square, but further to the west. When the new town hall was built in 1405, a new fixed structure developed in urban terms as well, and this shapes the layout of the city centre to the present day. It consists of a sequence of squares with the market place at its centre, retaining its central role as a kind of »forum«. Even though the west façade of the cathedral is not very far away, it was pushed aside somewhat by the skilful positioning of the town hall. The new town hall was placed on the axis of the old long-distance trade route, so that the street runs towards the narrow sides of the town hall and the large portals there for the lower hall from both the east and the west. The southern long side of the town hall takes up the entire north side of the market place as a closed frontage on the square, thus defining it in urban terms. This makes the town hall the dominant building in this central square. Adjacent to it – after short narrower sections in each case – are other squares: to the northeast is the Domshof, and to the north-west the Liebfrauenkirchhof. The right-hand flank is occupied by the old religious centre, the cathedral, and the left flank by the Ratskirche Unser Lieben Frauen. This arrangement was further developed when the merchants built the Schütting in 1537/38 to stand immediately opposite the town hall, as a headquarters for the representation of their interests. The west and east sides of the market place were occupied by small private houses with their gable sides to the street, definitely imposing, but in the form of detached structures on small parcels of land, in an additive series, thus created a subordinate link between the larger buildings. This built development created a frame around the market place that encouraged public use for key events. A court sat here, as well as the market activity, the council's decisions were proclaimed, ceremonies carried out and political demonstrations held. The market was and is a public centre of political significance.

The city continued to develop, acquired more parish churches and a medieval wall that was extended and reinforced in the 17th century. This secured the city's greatness. Historical views of the city in the 16th and 17th centuries show the situation very clearly. The town hall and the market form the urban centre. Distinct quarters developed around the parish churches, with bourgeois houses set gable-on to the street shaping the streetscape. The whole city was surrounded by urban fortifications that were given up in 1802 and turned into a public green space created by artistic garden designers, one of the earliest municipal parks. It was not until the mid 19th century that the city began to spill beyond these boundaries, especially as citizens' rights could now be held or retained outside the old city limits. Large quarters then emerged at the time of industrial expansion in the late 19th century, and the number of inhabitants rose to 125,000. This also brought about a change in the cityscape. Many families left their houses or offices in the old town, where they were replaced by large buildings such as stock exchanges, banks, post

risch gestaltete, öffentliche Grünanlage umwandelte, einen ersten frühen Bürgerpark. Erst in der Mitte des 19. Jahrhunderts begann die Stadt, sich stark über diese Grenzen hinaus zu vergrößern, besonders nachdem man das Bürgerrecht nun auch außerhalb der alten Stadtgrenzen innehaben bzw. behalten konnte. Danach entstanden bald große gründerzeitliche Quartiere, die Einwohnerzahl stieg gegen Ende des 19. Jahrhunderts auf 125 000 an. Dies brachte auch einen Wandel des Stadtbilds mit sich. Viele Familien verließen ihre Bürgerhäuser oder Kontore der Altstadt, wo sich stattdessen Großbauten wie Börsen, Banken, Post und Gerichte breitmachten. Auch der Marktplatz erfuhr 1861 eine einschneidende Veränderung, als die östliche Reihe der Bürgerhausbebauung einem monumentalen neogotischen Börsengebäude der Kaufmannschaft weichen musste. Nachdem dieses Gebäude im Zweiten Weltkrieg zerstört worden war, entstand nach heftiger öffentlicher Debatte 1962–66 nach Plänen von Wassili Luckhardt ein Parlamentsbau, das Haus der Bürgerschaft, das in Formen der modernen Architektursprache sich dem historischen Umfeld unterordnet. Somit ist auch die demokratische Kraft der Legislative am zentralen Platz der Freien Hansestadt Bremen angesiedelt, wo sich die gesellschaftlich relevanten Einrichtungen im Laufe der Geschichte städtebaulich vereint haben.

Baugeschichte des Rathauses

Die eigentliche Baugeschichte des Rathauses ist relativ geradlinig und dank einer guten Quellenlage (Chroniken und Rechnungsbücher) umfassend erforscht. Als der Beschluss des Rates erfolgt war, ein gänzlich neues Rathaus an anderer Stelle zu erbauen, begannen die Verhandlungen über den Bauplatz. Als erster Schritt im Gesamtkonzept stellte man 1404 den Roland auf, der eine ältere, vom Erzbischof 1366 zerstörte Rolandfigur ersetzte.

Die 5,55 m hohe strenge Statue ist das älteste und größte erhaltene Beispiel eines Rolandstandbilds. Rolande wurden auch an anderen Orten als Sinnbild für städtische Rechte aufgestellt. Die von einem Mantel umhüllte Figur besitzt Schwert und Gürtel, auf dessen Schnalle ein Engel und daneben eine Rose zu sehen sind. Roland, der als Paladin Kaiser Karls des Großen im Kampf gegen Ungläubige gefallen war, wird hier als Märtyrer, aber zugleich auch als Sendbote und Überbringer der vom Kaiser gewährten Freiheit dargestellt. Das wohl erst 1512 angebrachte Schild belegt mit seiner Inschrift diese Funktion zusätzlich. Der Roland ist damit die Bremer Freiheitsstatue.

Mit der Anfertigung der Rolandfigur müssen auch die Vorplanungen für das Rathaus begonnen haben. Durch den Abriss von Häusern und mit der Baustelleneinrichtung von Februar bis Mai 1405 leitete man schließlich konkrete Bauvorbereitungen ein. Seit dem 11. April 1405 arbeitete man bereits am Aushub der Grube für den Keller, und am 6. Mai 1405 wurden mit einer feierlichen Grundsteinlegung die Arbeiten am Bau offiziell begonnen. Die Ratsherren Hinrich von der Trupe und Friedrich Wigger trugen die Verantwortung für das Bauvorhaben. Von den Handwerkern sind die Maurermeister Salomon und Martin aus Bremen, der Steinmetzmeister Kurd aus Münster mit zehn Gesellen sowie ein Meister Westphal und die Bildhauermeister Johann – wie Kurd ebenfalls ein Auswärtiger – und Henning namentlich bekannt.

Während die Maurerarbeiten über den Winter eingestellt wurden, arbeiteten die Steinmetzen und Bildhauer in ihren Werkstätten ununterbrochen weiter. Schon Anfang 1406 waren die Sandsteinskulpturen für die Außenfassaden fertiggestellt, denn Henning und Johann erhielten hierfür im Frühjahr ihre Bezahlung.

Die ganze Baustelle muss bestens organisiert gewesen sein, denn es wird von reibungslosen Steinlieferungen per Schiff berichtet, die im Hafen anlandeten. Der Stein kam über die Weser aus Minden und wurde in Depots zur Verarbeitung vorgehalten. Im Frühjahr 1406 wurden die Maurerarbeiten wieder aufgenommen, und bis September war der Bau so weit fortgeschritten, dass die Zimmerleute mit dem Dachstuhl beginnen konnten. Das Dach wurde mit Ziegeln gedeckt, und im Jahr 1407 war der Rohbau vollständig fertiggestellt. Danach muss es wohl wegen neuerlicher Auseinandersetzungen mit dem Erzbischof zu Stockungen im Bauablauf gekommen sein. Erst 1410 arbeitete man wieder an der Innenausstattung. Das genaue Datum der Fertigstellung ist nicht bekannt.

Bildliche Darstellungen des Rathauses vor seinem Umbau im 17. Jahrhundert und die reichlich erhaltene originale Substanz lassen es zu, sich eine Vorstellung vom gotischen Gründungsbau zu machen. Das Städtebuch von Braun-Hogenberg: *Civitates Orbis Terrarum* von 1598 und zwei Abbildungen von Wilhelm Dilich aus *Urbis Bremae – Typus et chronicon* von 1602 und 1603 geben Aufschluss über den Umfang der Umbauarbeiten unter Lüder von Bentheim. Bereits davor gab es eine Veränderung, als 1532 der rückwärtige Zugang an der Nordseite, wo man über eine Freitreppe und ein gotisches Spitzbogenportal in die Obere Halle kam, vermauert wurde, um nach einem Aufstand eine bessere Zugangskontrolle zu schaffen. Dafür wurde eine Wendeltreppe im Inneren von der Unteren zur Oberen Halle eingebaut.

Bis zum Ende des 16. Jahrhunderts besaß das Rathaus gegenüber dem heutigen Zustand einige markante Besonderheiten: Dem Erdgeschoss war schon im gotischen Gründungsbau eine elfjochige Arkadenreihe vorgestellt, die jedoch Spitzbogen zeigte. Über den Scheiteln der Bögen verliefen ein Gesimsband, darüber ein vorspringender Zinnenkranz, eine Reihe Fenster und ein abschließendes Pultdach. Die Mitte des Vorbaus wurde durch eine höher aufragende und mit einem Dreiecksgiebel geschlossene Laube – wohl für Verkündigungen von Ratsbeschlüssen – akzentuiert. Die Fenster des Saalgeschosses waren ehedem spitzbogig, dazwischen befanden sich seit jeher große Sandsteinfiguren auf Konsolen mit Schutzbaldachinen. Darüber war eine Reihe von Rundmedaillons angeordnet, denen wiederum ein abschließender Zinnenkranz folgte, der den Anspruch der Wehrhaftigkeit zum Ausdruck brachte, aber ebenso architektonisch die Funktion der Attika, also der Kaschierung des Dachansatzes, übernahm. Die Gebäudeecken wurden von Achtecktürmchen auf Figurenkonsolen eingenommen. In der Nordwestecke hat sich diese gotische Eckgestaltung bis heute erhalten. Der Bau wurde von einem Walmdach bedeckt, das, wenn man den Bildquellen Glauben schenken darf, relativ flach geneigt gewesen war. Da der gesamte Kernbau mit seinen Figuren unverändert geblieben ist, sich an der Schmalseite die gotischen Fenster erhalten haben und auch eines der Ecktürmchen des 15. Jahrhunderts noch existiert, kann man sich ein recht gutes Bild vom gotischen Gründungsbau machen. Die Veränderungen, die folgten,

offices and courts. The market place also changed markedly in 1861, when the eastern row of residential properties had to make way for a monumental neo-Gothic stock exchange building for the merchants' corporation. After this building was destroyed in the Second World War, a parliament building was erected in 1962–66, after vigorous public debate and controversy. It is called the Haus der Bürgerschaft, and was built to plans by Wassili Luckhardt, and subordinated itself to its historical context while adopting the forms of modern architectural language. Thus the democratic power of the legislature is also based in the central square in the Free Hanseatic City of Bremen, where socially relevant facilities of come together in urban development terms with the passage of time.

The building history of the town hall

The actual building history of the town hall follows a relatively straight line and is comprehensively researched, thanks to excellent sources (chronicles and account books). Once the council had ordered a completely new town hall to be built in a different place, negotiations about the site began. The figure of Roland was erected in 1404, as the first step in the whole process. It replaced an older figure of Roland destroyed by the archbishop in 1366.

This austere piece is 5.55 m high, and the oldest and largest surviving example of a Roland statue. Rolands were also set up in other places to symbolize municipal rights. The figure is wrapped in a cloak. It has a sword and belt, with an angel and a rose on its buckle. Roland, who fell as a paladin of Charlemagne in the battle against the infidel, is represented here as a martyr but also at the same time as a messenger and bearer of the freedom guaranteed by the emperor. The shield was probably not added until 1512 and its inscription additionally confirms this function. This makes the Roland Bremen's statue of liberty.

Preliminary planning for the town hall must have started while the Roland was being completed. Concrete preparations for the operation began when houses were demolished and the building site set up from February to May 1405. Work was already in progress on excavating a pit for the cellar from 11 April 1405, and on 6 May 1405 building work began officially with a solemn laying of the foundation stone. Councillors Hinrich von der Trupe and Friedrich Wigger took responsibility for the building project. Of the craftsmen, master bricklayers Salomon and Martin of Bremen, master stonemason Kurd of Münster with ten journeymen as well as a Master Westphal and the master sculptors Johann – like Kurd an outsider as well – and Henning are known by name. While the bricklaying work was suspended in the winter months, the stonemasons and sculptors kept going in their workshops. Even in early 1406 the sandstone sculptures for the outer façades were completed; we know this because Henning and Johann were paid in the spring.

The entire building site must have been extremely well organized. There are reports of trouble-free deliver-

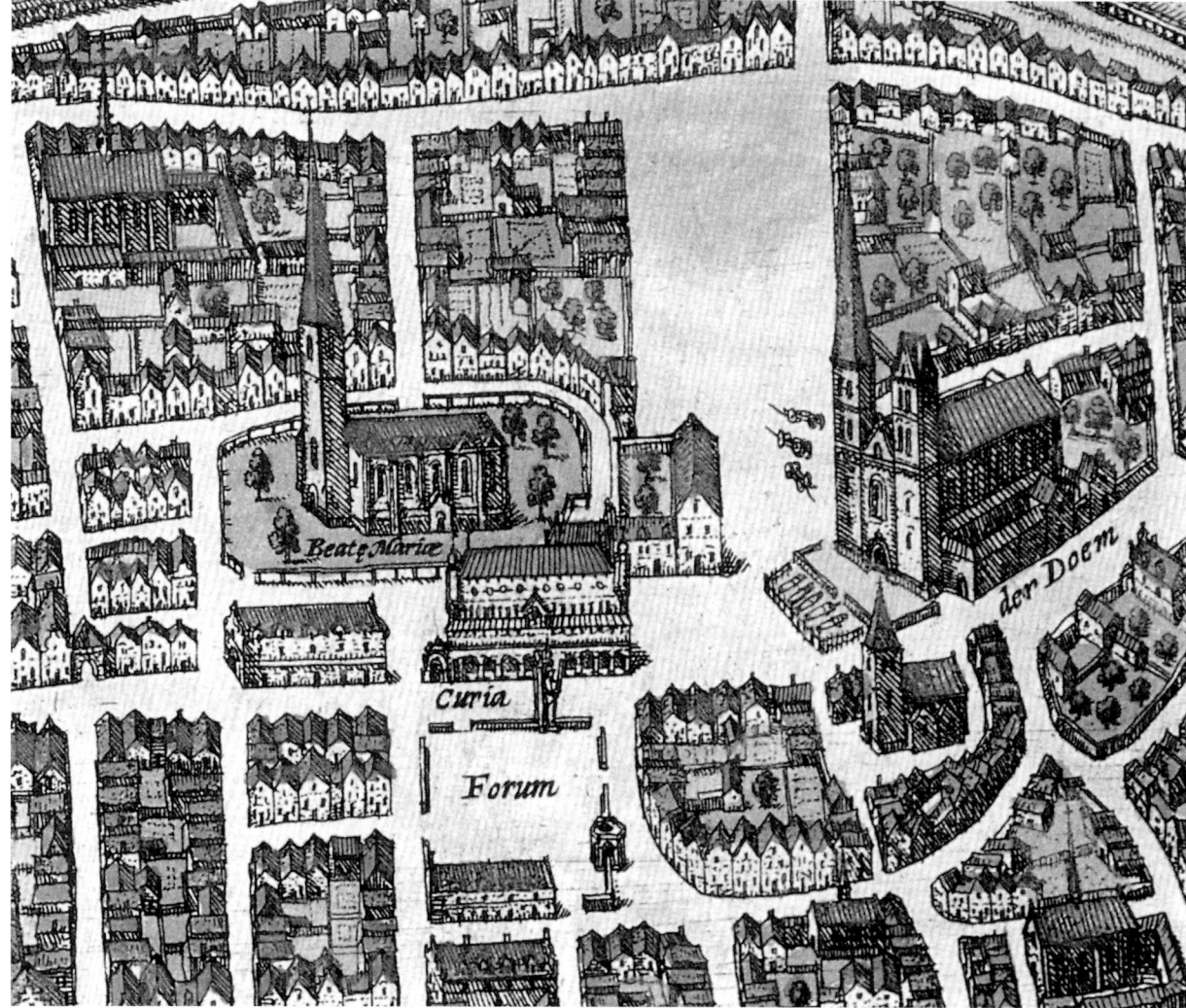

1. Georg Braun und Franz Hogenberg, *Civitates Orbis Terrarum*, 1598. Die städtebauliche Situation mit Marktplatz (»forum«) und Rathaus sowie den umgebenden Kirchen, Plätzen und Quartieren. (Staatsarchiv Bremen.)

1. Georg Braun und Franz Hogenberg, *Civitates Orbis Terrarum*, 1598. The urbanistic situation with market place (»forum«) and town hall as well as the surrounding churches, squares und quarters. (Staatsarchiv Bremen.)

waren zurückhaltend und sollten besonders ein erweitertes Bildprogramm und eine Fassade nach modernen Stilprinzipien mit sich bringen.

1595 wurde der Steinhauermeister Lüder von Bentheim beauftragt, die Fenster der Südseite zum Markt hin zu verbreitern. Es entstanden Rechteckfenster mit zeitgemäßen Renaissance-Verdachungen, mit abwechselnden Dreiecks- und Segmentbogengiebeln. Dies war der Auftakt zu Veränderungen, mit denen die Fassade – unter Beibehaltung des gotischen Kernbaus – in zeitgemäßen architektonischen Formen und mit einem aktualisierten ikonographischen Programm modernisiert wurde.

Die gesamte Maßnahme dauerte von 1608 bis 1614. Von Seiten des Rates waren Johann Wachmann und Heinrich Esig mit der Kontrolle der Arbeiten beauftragt.

1608 begann man mit einem neuen Dach. Der Zimmermannmeister Johann Stolling fertigte 1608/09 einen neuen mächtigen Dachstuhl, der 1611–13 in Kupfer gedeckt wurde. Trotz der inschriftlichen Datierung »1612« am östlichen Zwerchhaus dauerten die Arbeiten sicher bis 1614, denn für die Zeit von 1610 bis 1614 sind die Bildhauerarbeiten durch Lüder von Bentheim an der neuen Fassade archivalisch überliefert. Den Abschluss der Maßnahme bildeten die Verglasung der Fenster Anfang 1614 und ein kompletter Anstrich der Fassade Ende desselben Jahres.

Trotz verschiedener Restaurierungsmaßnahmen des 19. und 20. Jahrhunderts hat sich die Baugestalt von 1405 und 1614 im Wesentlichen bis zum heutigen Tag erhalten. Steinauswechslungen bei verschiedenen Reparaturmaßnahmen sind immer wieder in Anpassung an das Bestehende erfolgt. Einzig die heutige Farbfassung ist eine freie Erfindung und Zutat des frühen 20. Jahrhunderts, wie die farbigen Darstellungen des 17. Jahrhunderts belegen.

Die Umgestaltung von 1608 bis 1614 hatte deutliche Schwerpunkte. So war das neue mächtige Walmdach in Kupfer ein erheblicher Eingriff. Ebenso veränderte der große dreiachsige Mittelrisalit mit hohem Dreiecksgiebel die Südfassade maßgeblich. Damit erhielt der zuvor ruhige, lagernde querrechteckige Baukörper einen zentralen Kulminationspunkt. Dieser neue zentrale Akzent in der Fassade ruht auf den ebenfalls veränderten horizontalen Arkaden, die jetzt Rundbögen erhielten mit zwei übereinanderliegenden Brüstungsstreifen, welche Platz für Reliefs boten. Damit war eine zeitgemäße und aufwendige Marktfassade entstanden. Neben dem Wunsch, selbstbewusst und repräsentativ den Anspruch auf die Reichsunmittelbarkeit mit zeitgemäßen architektonischen, Mitteln zu unterstreichen, war die Fassadengestaltung auch eine direkte Reaktion auf den 1536–38 erbauten und 1594 aufwendig umgestalteten gegenüberliegenden Bau des Schütting, dem Gildehaus der Bremer Kaufleute.

Das Innere war von den Umbaumaßnahmen nur in Teilen betroffen. Der Ratskeller ist seit 1405 unverändert eine dreischiffige, elfjochige Halle mit Kappengewölben auf Steinpfeilern. Hier wurde von Anbeginn Wein gelagert, denn schon im 14. Jahrhundert hatte der Rat das Monopol auf den Verkauf von Rheinwein. Vom dreischiffigen Hauptraum des Kellers wurden im 19. Jahrhundert dreimal drei Joche abgetrennt, in denen Max Slevogt 1927 Fresken nach den *Phantasien im Bremer Ratskeller* von Wilhelm Hauff malte. Dem Kernbereich unter dem alten Rathaus sind heute weitere Kellerräume zugeordnet, so die unter den ehemaligen rückwärtigen Anbauten gelegenen alten Räume des Senats- und des Kaiserzimmers (1875 von Arthur Fitger dekoriert) und der Apostel- und Rosekeller, wo die ältesten erhaltenen Fassweine des 17. und 18. Jahrhunderts lagern. Nach Westen schließt sich der Raum des Bacchuskellers an, der ehedem das Kellergeschoss eines westlich vor dem Rathaus gelegenen Börsengebäudes des 17. Jahrhunderts war. Weitere Kellerräume liegen unter dem neuen Rathaus und unter dem Platz

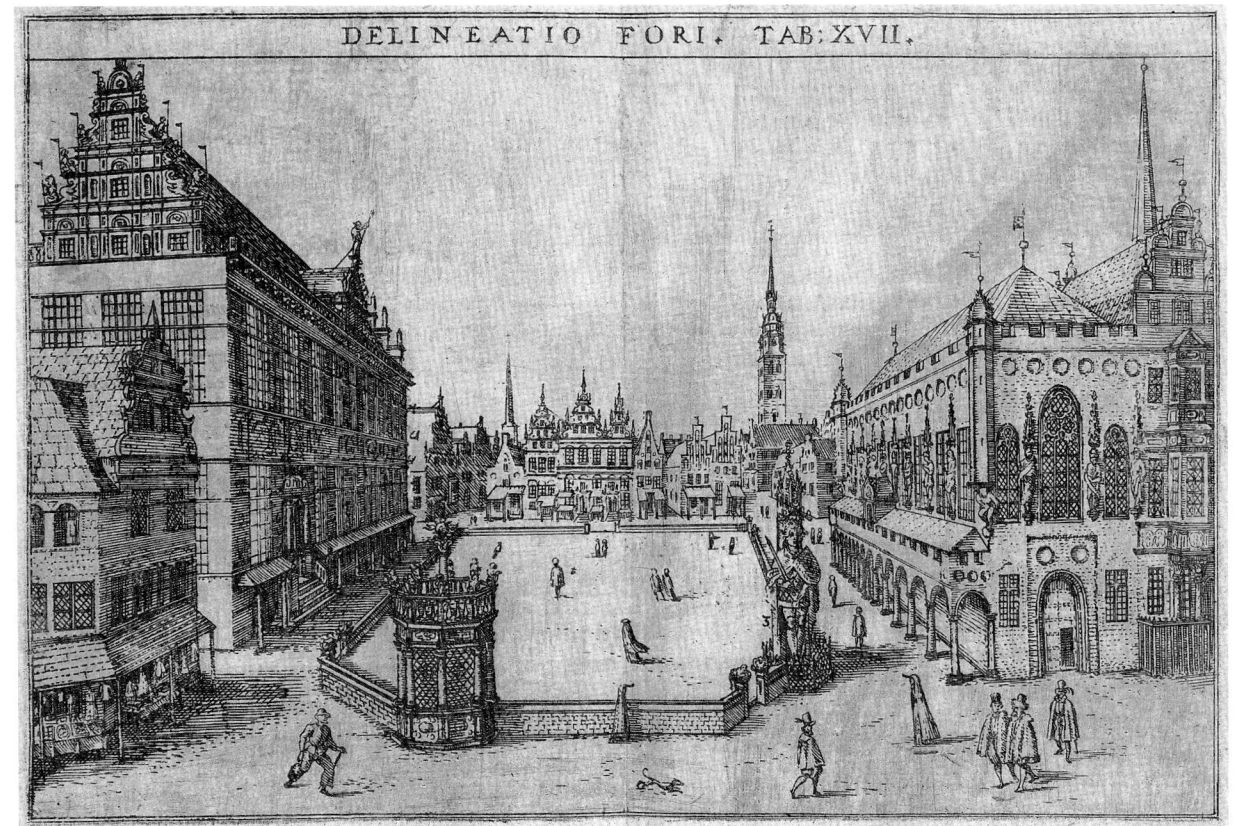

2. Wilhelm Dilich, *Urbis Bremae*, 1603. Es handelt sich um die einzige verlässliche Ansicht des gotischen Rathauses vor dem Umbau. Gut zu erkennen ist, dass die Fenster der Südfassade schon verändert sind. Die Zinnen, Tondi und Ecktürmchen prägen das Bild des oberen Fassadenabschlusses. (Staatsarchiv Bremen.)

2. Wilhelm Dilich, *Urbis Bremae*, 1603. This is the only reliable view of the Gothic town hall before the reconstruction. It is clear that the windows in the south façade have already been changed. The battlements, tondi and turrets mould the image of the upper façade conclusion. (Staatsarchiv Bremen.)

ies by ships arriving in the harbour. The stone came via the Weser from Minden, and was kept in depots before being worked on. Bricklaying work started again in spring 1406, and construction work had progressed so far by September that the carpenters were able to start work on the roof truss. The roof was covered with tiles and the shell was entirely completed by 1407. There must have been delays in the course of building after that because of recent clashes with the archbishop. Work on the interior was not taken up again until 1410. The exact completion date is not known.

Pictures of the town hall before it was modified in the 17th century and the original substance, which has survived to a considerable extent, make it possible to form an impression of the Gothic foundation building. The Braun-Hogenberg municipal book *Civitates Orbis Terrarum* of 1598 and two illustrations by Wilhelm Dillich from *Urbis Bremae – Typus et Chronicon* dating from 1602 and 1603 shed light on the extent of the modifications under Lüder von Bentheim. There was a change even before this, when the back entrance on the north side, which led into the upper hall via an open staircase and a portal with a pointed Gothic arch, was bricked up in 1532 to make it easier to control access after a revolt. A spiral staircase was installed inside, leading from the lower to the upper hall.

The town hall had some striking special feature in comparison with its present condition until the late 16th century: even in the original Gothic building there had been an eleven-bay arcade in front of the ground floor, but it had pointed arches. A cornice band ran along the tops of the arches, above this was a projecting run of battlements, a row of windows with a shed roof on the top. The middle of the building in front was accentuated by a taller arbour closed by triangular gables – probably for proclaiming the council's resolutions. The windows of the hall storey were formerly pointed, and between them there had always been large sandstone figures on pedestals and with protective baldachins. Above this was a row of round medallions, and these two were topped by a run of battlements expressing the building's claim to be able to defend itself, but also fulfilling the architectural function of the attic storey, in other words concealing the point at which the roof springs. The corners of the building were occupied by octagonal turrets on statue pedestals. This Gothic corner design has survived to the present day in the north-west corner. The building was topped by a hipped roof that must have had a quite shallow pitch, if the pictorial sources are to be believed. As the entire core building and its figures have remained unchanged, the Gothic windows have survived on the narrow side and one of the 15th century corner turrets still exists, it is possible to form a very good impression of the original Gothic building. The subsequent changes were restrained, intended mainly to introduce an extended pictorial programme and a façade based on modern stylistic principles.

In 1595, master stonehewer Lüder von Bentheim was commissioned to widen the windows facing the market place on the south side. This resulted in rectangular windows with Renaissance canopies appropriate to their day, alternating triangular and segmental-arched gables. This was the start of changes that led to the modernization of the façade – retaining the Gothic core building – using up-to-date architectural forms and also a modern iconographic programme.

The whole process lasted from 1608 to 1614. Johann Wachmann and Heinrich Esig were commissioned to oversee the work on the council side.

A start was made on a new roof in 1608. Master carpenter Johann Stolling constructed a massive new roof truss in 1608/09, and this was clad in copper in 1611 to 1613. Despite the date inscription »1612« on the east dormer, the work certainly continued until 1614, as there is archival evidence for work by Lüder von Bentheim on sculptures for the new façade from 1610 to 1614. The project was concluded with the glazing of the windows early in 1614, and by the painting of the entire façade in late 1614.

Despite various pieces of restoration work in the 19th and 20th centuries, the shape of the building as in 1405 and 1614 has largely survived to the present day. Where stone has been replaced in the course of various repairs, it has always been matched with the existing material. Only today's colour scheme is a free invention and addition dating from the early 20th century, as shown by 17th century coloured pictorial material.

There were clear key guidelines for the change of design from 1608 to 1614. So the massive new hip roof was a considerable intervention. In the same way, the large central projecting section with three axes and a tall triangular marked a substantial change for the south façade. It gave the building, hitherto calmly horizontal and rectangular, a central culmination point. This new central accent in the façade is based on the horizontal arcades, which have also been changed: they acquires round arches with two parapet strips, one above the other, offering space for reliefs. This created an elaborate façade on the market place side that was appropriate to its times. As well as a desire to underline the claim to imperial immediacy self-confidently and imposingly with up-to-date architectural resources, the façade design was also responding to the Schütting, the Bremen merchants' guild building opposite, erected in 1536–38 and elaborately redesigned in 1594.

The interior was affected by the reconstruction only in part. The Ratskeller has been unchanged since 1405 as a hall with three aisles and eleven bays, with cap vaults on stone piers. Wine was stored here from the outset: even in the 14th century the council has a monopoly on the sales of Rhenish wines. In the 19th century, three times three bays were separated off from the three aisles of the main room in the Ratskeller. Max Slevogt painted frescos on these in 1927, based on the Wilhelm Hauff's *Phantasien im Bremer Ratskeller*. More cellar space has been allotted to the core area under the old town hall today, including the old Senatszimmer and the Kaiserzimmer (decorated by Arthur Fitger in 1875) under the former rear extensions, and the Apostelkeller and the Rosekeller, where the oldest surviving 17th and 18th century wines in barrels are stored. The Bacchuskeller is adjacent on the west side. This used to be the cellar of a 17th century stock exchange building west of the town hall. Other cellar spaces are to be found under the new town hall and the Domhof square. The Bremen Ratskeller's most valuable wines are kept in the »Schatzkammer« here.

The ground floor of the town hall, the lower hall, with three aisles and eleven bays like the Ratskeller, is divided up by oak stands. It was used as a merchants' hall. Here too the 1405 conditions are maintained to the greatest possible extent. Above is the upper hall, where council meetings used to be held, but it was also used

des Domhofs. Hier werden heute die wertvollsten Weine des Bremer Ratskellers in der »Schatzkammer« aufbewahrt.

Das Erdgeschoss des Rathauses, die Untere Halle, wie der Ratskeller ebenfalls dreischiffig und elfjochig, wird von Eichenholzständern unterteilt. Sie diente als Kaufhalle. Auch hier ist der Zustand von 1405 weitestgehend erhalten. Darüber liegt die Obere Halle, wo Ratssitzungen stattfanden, aber auch Gericht gehalten und Feste gefeiert wurden. Die Obere Halle ist möglicherweise seit dem Mittelalter ungeteilt und stützenlos, was bei einer Größe von 41 x 16 m eine enorme bautechnische Leistung darstellt. Als innenräumliches Gegenstück zum neu geschaffenen Mittelrisalit wurde hier 1612–19 ein zweigeschossiger hölzerner Einbau eingestellt, die Güldenkammer. Sie trägt ihren Namen nach der vergoldeten Ledertapete, die den Raum auskleidete. Zur Oberen Halle zeigt sich die Güldenkammer als reich verziertes Meisterstück der Renaissance-Schnitzkunst. Wahrscheinlich wurden die Arbeiten vom Ratszimmermeister Reinecke Stolling und seinen Gehilfen ausgeführt. Der untere Teil der Güldenkammer wurde 1905 nach Entwürfen des Worpsweder Künstlers Heinrich Vogeler als Sitzungszimmer neu ausgestaltet: ein Gesamtkunstwerk mit Jugendstilanklängen, bei dem von der Türklinke über den Kamin, die Lampen, die Wanddekoration und das Mobiliar alles aufeinander abgestimmt ist.

Weitere Maßnahmen beschränkten sich auf kleinere Veränderungen an der Ausstattung und besonders auf einen rückwärtigen Erweiterungsbau. Nach erheblicher Zunahme der Verwaltungsaufgaben am Ende des 19. Jahrhunderts beschloss der Rat der Stadt, kein neues großes Rathaus an der Stelle des alten zu erbauen, wie dies in vielen Städten in Deutschland um 1900 der Fall war, sondern das historische Rathaus geschickt zu erweitern. Auf den von Gabriel von Seidl kurz vor dem Ersten Weltkrieg ausgeführten Anbau des Neuen Rathauses ist später noch einzugehen.

Zur Bautypologie

Die bisherige Forschung hat sich sehr intensiv mit der Entschlüsselung und der Analyse des Bildprogramms der Fassade beschäftigt. Bauhistorische Untersuchungen zur Provenienz der hier verwendeten typologischen Formen wie der Architekturdetails sind noch nicht im gleichen Umfang betrieben worden. Dabei scheint es offensichtlich auch programmatisch gewesen zu sein, welche Bauten und Kulturlandschaften Anregungen zum gotischen Rathausbau und zur Veränderung der Renaissance gegeben haben.

Der gotische Rathausbau von 1405 wurde bereits mit hohem Anspruch entwickelt. Allein die Größe von 41 x 16 m ist für ein Rathaus dieser Zeit außergewöhnlich. Aber auch an der Wahl einzelner Formen glaubt man, sehr deutlich eine Orientierung an ganz besonderen Vorbildern festzustellen. Zunächst muss festgehalten werden, dass man für das Rathaus als klar ausgebildeten Rechteckbau mit Keller, Markthalle im Erdgeschoss und dem großen repräsentativen Saal im Obergeschoss die reine, unverfälschte Grundform des »Saalgeschossbaus«, wie er typisch für mittelalterliche Rathäuser ist, gewählt hat. Seit dem frühen Mittelalter hat sich dieser Typus für herrschaftliche Residenzbauten herausgebildet. Aus der Aula regia der römischen Kaiserzeit entwickelten sich in karolingischer Zeit der Palas und die

3. Matthaeus Merian, *Topographia Germaniae, Saxoniae Inferioris*, 1653, Reprint Kassel 1960 ff. Merian hat offenbar Dilichs Stich zur Grundlage genommen und nur die Veränderungen am Rathaus eingearbeitet. Insofern liegt hier nur eine eingeschränkte Verlässlichkeit vor.
4. Erik Dahlberg, 1667. Die dominante Wirkung und zentrale Stellung des Rathauses am Marktplatz wird auch hier hervorgehoben. (Staatsarchiv Bremen.)

3. Matthaeus Merian, *Topographia Germaniae, Saxoniae Inferioris*, 1653, reprint Kassel 1960 ff. Merian obviously used Dilich's engraving as a basis and simply worked in the changes to the town hall. In this respect the image is reliable to only a limited extent.
4. Erik Dahlberg, 1667. The dominant effect and central position of the town hall in the market place is emphasized here as well. (Staatsarchiv Bremen.)

for court sittings and festivities. The upper hall may have been undivided and column-free since the middle ages, which represents an enormous technical achievement given that it measures 41 x 16 m. The Güldenkammer, an interior counterpart to the newly created central projecting section was added here in 1612–19 in the form of a two-storey timber insertion. Its name relates to the gilded leather wallpaper in which the room used to be clad. The Güldenkammer appears as a richly decorated masterpiece of the Renaissance carver's art on the upper-hall side. The work was probably carried out by council master carpenter Reinecke Stolling and his assistants. The lower section of the Güldenkammer was redesigned as a meeting room in 1905 by the Worpswede artist Heinrich Vogeler. A *Gesamtkunstwerk* with hints of Jugendstil, in which everything from the door latch via the fireplace, the lamps, the wall decoration and the furniture represents a matching work of art.

Other measures were restricted to minor changes to the furnishings and especially to the extension at the back. The council was faced with a considerably greater number of administrative tasks in the late 19th century, and so it decided not to replace the old town hall with a new one, which happened in a large number of German towns around 1900, but to extend the historic town hall as skilfully as possible. The new town hall extension, built by Gabriel von Seidl shortly before the First World War, will be discussed later.

About the typology of the building

Previous research has concentrated very hard on decoding and analysing the pictorial programme on the façade. So far there have been no investigations on a similar scale in terms of architectural history about the provenance of the typological forms used here or the architectural details. But there seems to have been a programme here too relating to which buildings and cultural landscapes affected the building of the Gothic town hall and the changes at the time of the Renaissance.

The 1405 Gothic town hall building was developed with high ambitions even then. Its size alone, 41 x 16 m. is extraordinary for a town hall of this period. But it also seems possible to see an orientation towards quite particular models expressed in the choice of individual forms. First of all, it must be remembered that the pure and unadulterated basic form of the »hall building with more than one storey«, typical of medieval town halls, was chosen for Bremen town hall as a clearly formed rectangular structures with cellar, market hall on the ground floor and a large, prestigious hall on the upper floor. This type evolved for rulers' residences from the early middle ages. The great hall and the king's hall developed from the aula regia of the imperial Roman age in the Caroligian era. The West Gothic aula regia of Ramiros I (Santa Maria del Naranco), built around 850, is one of the few surviving early examples that shows this form in its fully developed state. A lucid rectangular structure without special accents has a large hall accessible by an open staircase from the outside on the upper floor, with a low ground floor below. The sole purpose of this upper floor is to have a higher – in both senses of the word – assembly room. This basic type can also be found in the Carolingian royal palaces and later also in the castles of the nobility. The imperial palaces at Aachen (8th century), Ingelheim (8th century) and Goslar (11th century) as well as castles like the Wartburg (12th century), Gelnhausen (12th century) or Dankwarderode (12th century) all have or had a typically configured, imposing great hall. Just as emperors, kings and princes proclaimed resolutions, held assemblies or administered the law in the great hall, this building type was also ideally suited for the work of administrative centres in the self-governed cities that had emerged since the 12th century. This political form of the independent city community came into being in Italy, where the Palazzo Publico or Palazzo Communale appeared increasingly as a building type from the 13th century onwards. Both the urban positioning, as a rule a dominant site by the market place – usually occupying one whole side – and the architectural form of the hall building are shared by numerous examples. The façade forms correspond with the taste of the time in question: the ground floors had either open arcades or portals and windows, in the early days with pointed arches in each case. The halls on the upper floor were lit by large windows with pointed arched, with the even arrangement of the windows and a clear order for the façade as striking features even at an early stage. And almost all the examples in northern and central Italy show the special design feature of the upper façade topped by a run of battlements projecting above consoles and corner accentuations, often by turrets. These battlements have of course absolutely no functional significance, but symbolize the city's ability to defend itself. It is precisely

Königshalle. Die westgotische Aula regia Ramiros I. (Santa Maria del Naranco), um 850 erbaut, ist eines der wenigen erhaltenen frühen Beispiele, das diese Form bereits voll ausgeprägt zeigt. Ein klarer Rechteckbau ohne besondere Akzentuierungen besitzt über einem niedrigen Erdgeschoss eine große Halle im Obergeschoss, die von außen über eine Freitreppe zugänglich ist. Der einzige Zweck des Obergeschosses ist, einen – im wahrsten Sinne des Wortes – herausgehobenen Versammlungssaal zu beherbergen. Dieser Grundtypus findet sich auch in den karolingischen Pfalzen und ebenso später bei Adelsburgen. Die kaiserlichen Pfalzen von Aachen (8. Jahrhundert), Ingelheim (8. Jahrhundert) und Goslar (11. Jahrhundert) sowie Burgen wie die Wartburg (12. Jahrhundert), Gelnhausen (12. Jahrhundert) oder Dankwarderode (12. Jahrhundert) besitzen oder besaßen einen typisch ausgebildeten, repräsentativen Palas. So wie Kaiser, Könige und Fürsten im Palas Beschlüsse verkündeten, Versammlungen abhielten oder Recht sprachen, war dieser Bautypus auch bestens geeignet für die Aufgaben eines Verwaltungszentrums der sich seit dem 12. Jahrhundert herausbildenden selbstverwalteten Städte. Diese politische Form der selbstständigen Stadtkommune entstand in Italien, wo der Bautypus Palazzo Pubblico oder Palazzo Communale ab dem 13. Jahrhundert verstärkt auftritt. Sowohl die städtebauliche Stellung, in der Regel eine dominante Position am Marktplatz – meist eine ganze Platzseite einnehmend – wie auch die architektonische Form des Saalgeschossbaus zeichnen zahlreiche Beispiele gemeinsam aus. Entsprechend dem Geschmack der jeweiligen Zeit zeigt sich die Formenausbildung der Fassade: Die Erdgeschosse besaßen entweder geöffnete Arkadengänge oder Portale und Fenster, in der Frühzeit jeweils mit Spitzbögen. Die Säle des Obergeschosses wurden durch große spitzbogige Fenster belichtet, wobei schon früh eine gleichmäßige Reihung der Fenster und eine klare Ordnung der Fassade auffallen. Ebenso zeigen nahezu alle Beispiele in Ober- und Mittelitalien die besondere Gestaltung des oberen Fassadenabschlusses durch einen über Konsolen vorkragenden Zinnenkranz und Eckakzentuierungen, oftmals durch Türmchen. Diese Zinnen besitzen natürlich keinerlei tatsächliche funktionale Bedeutung, sondern stehen symbolhaft für die Wehrhaftigkeit der Stadt. Genau diese Details sind es, die eine mittel- oder unmittelbare Orientierung des gotischen Rathauses von Bremen an italienischen Vorbildern vermuten lassen. Die klare, regelmäßige Rechteckform mit gleichmäßig gereihten Fenstern war für Mitteleuropa um 1400 noch ungewöhnlich. Auch der gleichmäßige Arkadengang vor der Fassade kann an italienischen Beispielen orientiert sein, ebenso wie die horizontale Bänderung (in Bremen mit roten und schwarzen Ziegeln) ein Motiv ist, das die italienische Architektur der Zeit häufig auszeichnet. Der wehrhafte Zinnenkranz und die Reihung von Tondi, das relativ flache Walmdach sowie die Größe und Gleichmäßigkeit der Saalfenster finden sich in vergleichbarer Art an italienischen Rathäusern. Auch die schon erwähnte städtebauliche Stellung – das Rathaus nimmt die ganze Seite eines Platzes ein, der in Bremen von den Zeitgenossen bezeichnenderweise »Forum« genannt wird – verweist auf italienische Einflüsse. Das italienische System der selbstverwalteten Stadt hat den Bremer Ratsherren möglicherweise ebenso als Vorbild gedient wie die dazugehörigen Bauten, so der Palazzo della Ragione in Padua (1219), der Broletto Nuovo in Mailand (1233) oder besonders der Palazzo Comunale in Piacenza (1280) und der Palazzo dei Priori in Perugia (1293).

Die für die nordeuropäische Rathausentwicklung architekturgeschichtlich besondere Stellung des gotischen Rathausbaus von 1405, der, wie ausgeführt, sich nahezu vollständig erhalten hat, kann an dieser Stelle nur angedeutet werden. Andere bedeutende mittelalterliche Rathausbauten Deutschlands, die allerdings allesamt verloren sind, folgten zum Teil ebenfalls vergleichbaren Grundideen. Sie können, wenn sie älter waren, wie zum Beispiel in Aachen, Nürnberg und Köln, durchaus auch Einflüsse auf Bremen ausgeübt haben. Für Bremen scheint jedoch eine unmittelbare Beeinflussung aus Italien erfolgt zu sein.

Durch den Umbau des gotischen Rathauses in den Jahren 1608 bis 1616 wurde mit vergleichsweise geringem Aufwand eine vollkommen veränderte architektonisch-künstlerische Aussage getroffen. Hatte man zuvor ein Rathaus mit demonstrativ republikanischer Stadtarchitektur italienischer Prägung, wählte man jetzt, im Sinne des aufkommenden Reichsstils, Kunstströmungen, die vom Prager Kaiserhof ausgingen.

Um 1600 entwickelte sich um den kunstbeflissenen Kaiser Rudolf II., der von 1576 bis 1612 regierte, und seinen Nachfolger Matthias am Prager Kaiserhof ein neues Verständnis für und eine neue Art des Umgangs mit Architektur. Die Bauten erhielten jetzt noch stärker demonstrativ-programmatische Aussagen. So errichteten bzw. finanzierten die protestantischen Fürsten des Reiches 1609–13 an der Prager Kleinseite eine Lutherische Dreifaltigkeitskirche, die dem Majestätsbrief von 1609 zufolge als politische Machtdemonstration zu begreifen ist.

Die Planung erfolgte durch die kaiserlichen Hofbaumeister Josef Heintz und Giovanni Maria Filippi. Dabei wählten die Künstler als exaktes Vorbild die katholische Dreifaltigkeitskirche S. Trinità dei Monti in Rom. Das Kopieren bzw. die starke Beeinflussung durch einen bestehenden Bau ist eine neue Zeitströmung. Um 1600 fand eine intensive gegenseitige Beeinflussung im Kunstschaffen statt. Durch Bildungsreisen der Bauherren und Architekten nach Italien und Frankreich, besonders aber auch durch die hohe Verbreitung zahlreicher neuer Architekturtraktate, Topographien, Muster- und Vorlagenbücher erlebte die Architektur eine Art ersten internationalen Stil. Die Verarbeitung von Anregungen bestehender Bauten oder aus Traktaten war nicht Ausdruck von Einfallslosigkeit, sondern demonstrativer Beweis für höchste Gelehrsamkeit und akademischen Bildungsstand sowie ein Garant für künstlerische Qualität. So ist im frühen 17. Jahrhundert die Umgestaltung der Fassade des Bremer Rathauses als eine Art Empfehlung an den Kaiser und ein Stück Reichsverbundenheit zu verstehen. Mit der Herausbildung des mächtigen dreiachsigen und übergiebelten Mittelrisalits erhielt das Rathaus eine schlossartige, akzentuierte Fassadenmitte als zentralen Kulminationspunkt der Architektur, ähnlich einer antikisierenden Tempelfront, die häufig bei anderen repräsentativen Bauten der italienischen Hochrenaissance anzutreffen ist. Der Mittelrisalit in Bremen hat keinen Bezug zu Ausluchten oder Lauben, wie sie die Schlösser der Weserrenaissance, etwa in Lemgo oder Paderborn, besitzen. Die Grundstruktur der Architektur mit italienisierendem, rundbogigem Arkadengang, mächtigem zentralen Mittelrisalit, Attikabalustrade und Rechteckfenstern mit Renaissance-Verdachungen fungiert als eine Art Bildträger für einen darauf aufgebrachten manieristi-

5. Paul Koster, *Chronik der Kaiserlichen Freien Reichs- und Hansestadt Bremen*, 1683. Farbige Fassung des Rathauses nach dem Renaissance-Umbau. (Staatsarchiv Bremen.)

5. Paul Koster, *Chronik der Kaiserlichen Freien Reichs- und Hansestadt Bremen*, 1683. Coloured representation of the town hall after the conversion in the Renaissance. (Staatsarchiv Bremen.)

these details that give rise to the supposition that Bremen's Gothic town hall was influenced directly or indirectly by Italian models. The clear, regular rectangular form with even rows of windows was as yet unusual for Central Europe around 1400. Even the regular arcade in front of the façade could well derive from Italian examples, and equally the horizontal banding (using red and black bricks in Bremen) is a motif that frequently characterizes the Italian architecture of the day. The defensive battlements and the row of tondi, the relatively shallow hip roof and the size and evenness of the hall windows can be found in comparable form in Italian town halls. And the above-mentioned urban positioning – the town hall occupies one whole side of the square, which contemporaries in Bremen significantly called a »forum« – suggests Italian influence. The Bremen councillors may also have taken the Italian self-governing city system as a model, as well as the buildings associated with it, such as the Palazzo della Ragione in Padua (1219), the Broletto Nuovo in Milan (1233) or in particular the Palazzo Comunale in Piacenza (1280) and the Palazzo dei Priori in Perugia (1293).

It is not possible to explore in full here the special position occupied by the Gothic town hall of 1405, which, as has already been stated, has survived almost in its entirety, for the development of the northern European town hall in terms of architectural history. Other important medieval town halls in Germany, all of which are lost, incidentally, followed similar basic ideas, to some extent. If they were older, like for example Aachen, Nuremberg and Cologne, they could have influenced Bremen town hall as well. But Bremen certainly does seem to have been influenced directly by Italy.

The modification of the Gothic town hall from 1608 to 1616 achieved a completely different architectural and artistic statement with comparatively little effort. Previously the people of Bremen had a town hall with demonstratively republican urban architecture shaped by Italian models, but now, in the spirit of the up-and-coming style of the empire, Bremen chose artistic trends emanating from the imperial court in Prague.

In about 1600, the emperor Rudolf II, who reigned from 1576 to 1612, and was zealous in his pursuit of art, and his successor Matthias developed a new understanding of and a new way of handing architecture at the Prague imperial court. The buildings now made even stronger demonstrative and programmatic statements. For example, from 1609 to 1613 the Protestant princes of the empire built or financed a Lutheran church of the Trinity on the Kleinseite in Prague. This is to be seen as a demonstration of political power as a consequence of the 1609 Letter of Majesty.

Planning was carried out by imperial master builders Josef Heintz and Giovanni Maria Filippi. The artists chose the Catholic church of S. Trinità dei Monti in Rome as an exact model. Copying, or powerful influence by an existing building, is a new trend in this period. A high level of mutual influence in the sphere of artistic creativity began around 1600. Clients and architects undertook educational trips to Italy and France, architectural treatises, topographies, and pattern and model books were disseminated in enormous numbers, and this meant that architecture acquired a kind of early international style. Working with ideas from existing buildings or treatises did not express a paucity of ideas, but demonstrated the highest level of scholarship and academic education, and also guaranteed artistic quality. So in the early 17th century the new design for the façade of Bremen town hall is to be seen as a kind of compliment to the emperor and a sign of commitment to the empire. The development of the powerful central projection with its three axes and gables at the top gave the town hall a palace-like, accentuated centre to its

schen Schmuck norddeutsch-niederländischer Prägung. Derartige Dekorationsformen wurden unter anderem über den in den Niederlanden geborenen Maler und Stecher Hans Vredeman de Vries verbreitet. Durch die Anstellung von Vredeman de Vries am Kaiserhof in Prag unter Rudolf II. avancierte diese Dekorationskunst zum Hofstil, der wiederum ins gesamte Reich ausstrahlte und von dessen Regenten aufgenommen wurde.

Das Bremer Rathaus ist sowohl in seiner Erstform des gotischen Gründungsbaus wie in seiner Modernisierung des 17. Jahrhunderts höchst programmatisch entwickelt worden. Zunächst zeigt es Verbindungen zu den frühen italienischen Stadtrepubliken und ihren selbstbewussten Verwaltungsbauten, sodann zum kaiserlichen Hof in Prag.

Ikonographie

Das gesamte Rathaus war neben seiner architektonischen Aussage auch Träger für weitere bildliche Ausgestaltungen mit politisch-programmatischem Anspruch. Schon das gotische Rathaus besaß an der Fassade den großen Figurenzyklus mit den Bildnissen des Kaisers und der sieben Kurfürsten. Die etwa lebensgroßen Figuren sind durch Wappenschilde bzw. Reichsinsignien klar identifiziert. Von links reihen sich auf: der Kaiser, die geistlichen Kurfürsten von Mainz, Trier und Köln und die weltlichen Regenten von Böhmen, Rhein-Pfalz, Sachsen und Brandenburg. Der Bremer Rat huldigte nicht dem Landesherrn, sondern dem Kaiser und stellte sich somit in eine Reihe mit den Kurfürsten und bezeugte damit bereits ein reichsstädtisches Selbstbewusstsein. Weitere Figuren an den Schmalseiten sind der Stadtpatron Petrus – zum Dom ausgerichtet – sowie alttestamentarische Propheten, die als Mahner für Gerechtigkeit stehen. Über die übrige mittelalterliche Ausgestaltung der Fassade liegen keine weiteren Informationen vor, die Wappenschilde und Tondi sind verloren.

Die Umgestaltung der Fassade in der Zeit von 1608 bis 1616 behielt den Kaiser- und Kurfürstenzyklus bei, da die damit getätigte Aussage unverändert Gültigkeit hatte. Hinzu kam jetzt aber ein höchst anspruchsvolles, aufwendiges und gelehrtes Bildprogramm in Form von Reliefs auf den eigens dafür geschaffenen Flächen. Dargestellt sind Tugenden, Sinne, Künste, Elemente, Jahreszeiten und anderes, wodurch die Fassade geradezu zu einem enzyklopädischen Gesamtbild entwickelt wird. In den vom Marktplatz aus gut erkennbaren 22 Zwickeln der Arkaden sind additiv die Eigenschaften und Tugenden aufgelistet, die den Rat auszeichnen: Philosophie, Wahrheit, Wachsamkeit, Obhut, Arbeit, Fleiß, Freigebigkeit, Stärke, Großmut, Eintracht, Geduld, Keuschheit, Besonnenheit, Gedächtnis, Glaube, Hoffnung, Fürsorge, Gerechtigkeit, Mäßigung, Klugheit, Friede und Ruhm. In den Friesen der Gebälkstücke des Mittelrisalits finden sich jeweils Figurenpaare, die die Sinne (Gesicht, Gehör, Geruch, Geschmack, Gefühl) und die Künste (Grammatik, Dialektik, Rhetorik, Musik, Arithmetik, Geometrie, Astronomie) sowie noch einmal Tugenden (Liebe, Glaube, Klugheit, Hoffnung, Gerechtigkeit, Friede, Stärke und Mäßigung) und die Elemente (Feuer, Wasser, Erde und Luft) symbolisieren. Ergänzt wird das Fassadenprogramm durch die Jahreszeiten, Planeten, Evangelisten und die sogenannten Seelenkämpfe (Psychomachien). Abgeschlossen wird der Bau durch vollplastische Freifiguren in der Dachzone, als Eckakroterien sowie als Bekrönungen der Giebel der Zwerchhäuser und des Mittelrisalits. Hier finden sich Krieger und zum wiederholten Male die Tugenden.

Sinn der Darstellungen ist die Verherrlichung des regierenden Rates, eine Art panegyrische Selbstdarstellung, wie sie in dieser Zeit auch bei anderen Herrschaftsbauten häufig anzutreffen ist. Die Stadtfreiheit sowie die Ziele des Gemeinwohls und der Gerechtigkeit für diese Stadt werden in Architektur und Bildausstattung zum Ausdruck gebracht.

Die Ikonographie setzt sich auch im Inneren fort. Die großen Wandgemälde von Bartholomäus Bruyn von 1532 zeigen den Gründungsakt der Stadt, als Kaiser Karl der Große Bischof Willehad den Dom übergibt, ein Hinweis auf die Kaiserfreiheit der Stadt und das salomonische Urteil, das als Mahnung zur Gerechtigkeit zu verstehen ist. Die Holzschnitzereien der Güldenkammer führen die am Außenbau angeschlagenen Themen weiter. Planeten, Gottheiten und Krieger schmücken die Brüstung der Treppe. Neben Reliefs mit den Sinnen und Tugenden zieren als vollplastische Figuren Herkules die Treppenspindel und Justitia mit Kriegern sowie das von Löwen getragene Bremer Wappen das Portal. In die Wände der Güldenkammer zur Oberen Halle sind Gemälde mit Gerechtigkeitsdarstellungen eingelassen.

Für die Darstellungen am Rathaus lassen sich mittelbare und unmittelbare Vorbilder aus unterschiedlichen Stichwerken benennen, ein Beleg dafür, mit welch hohem Kenntnisstand und welcher Bildungsbeflissenheit die Verantwortlichen das Rathaus ausgestaltet wissen wollten.

Der Roland

Obwohl die Monumentalfigur des Rolands auf dem Marktplatz losgelöst vor dem Rathaus steht, ist sie untrennbar mit diesem verbunden. Als erster Akt des Gesamtprojekts ist die Figur 1404 auf dem Marktplatz aufgestellt worden, möglicherweise auch als eine Art Verkünder dessen, was sich mit dem Neubau des Rathauses ändern sollte, sicherlich jedoch bringt er das neue Selbstbewusstsein der politisch unabhängig handelnden Ratsherrschaft zum Ausdruck. Die legendäre Person des Roland, der zum Gefolge Karls des Großen gehörte, steht immer wieder ganz allgemein als allegorisches Zeichen für Markt- und Freiheitsrechte der Städte. Etwa 40 Rolande existieren noch heute, der Bremer ragt aus den erhaltenen in mehrfacher Hinsicht heraus: Es ist die älteste, größte und künstlerisch bedeutendste Figur dieser Art, und da sie fast freistehend ist – sie besitzt nur eine schmale Stütze im Rücken, die den sie schützenden gotischen Baldachin trägt –, ist sie zugleich eine der ältesten Freifiguren nördlich der Alpen. Die besondere Strenge der Darstellung und die Höhe der Figur von über 5 m heben sie heraus. Rolande stehen oft allgemein für die Marktrechte, der Bremer Roland wird jedoch sehr konkret in seiner Aussage: Durch seine Gürtelschnalle, die einen Laute spielenden Engel darstellt, und durch die Rose am Gürtel ist er als Märtyrer gekennzeichnet und damit als der konkrete historische Roland, Markgraf der Bretagne, zu verstehen, der im Gefolge des Kaisers unterwegs war. Somit ist er der reale Bote Karls des Großen, der hier die Kaiserfreiheit als bedeutendes Sonderrecht Bremens überbringt. Der Schild – der jetzige stammt von 1512 – erläutert dies noch konkreter: »vryheit do ik ju openbar de karl ... des-

façade as the central culmination point of the architecture, similar to an ancient temple façade, a form that occurs frequently in other imposing Italian Renaissance buildings. The central projecting section in Bremen does not relate to oriels or arbours of the kind found in Weser Renaissance palaces like Lemgo or Paderborn. The basic structure of the architecture with its Italianate, round-arched arcade, powerful central projecting section, attic balustrade and rectangular windows with Renaissance roofing functions as a kind of picture support for the typically north German-Dutch Mannerist decoration that is applied to it. Decorative forms of this kind were disseminated by painters and engravers including Hans Vredeman de Vries, who was born in Holland. Vredeman de Vries's appointment to the imperial court in Prague under Rudolf II raised this decorative art to the status of a court style. This spread out all over the empire in its turn and was taken up by its rulers.

Bremen town hall was developed according to a programme to a high degree, both in its original Gothic form and its 17th century modernization. First it showed links with the Italian city republics and their confident government buildings, then with the imperial court in Prague.

Iconography

The entire town hall made an architectural statement, but it also carried further pictorial elements of a political and programmatic nature. Even the Gothic town hall had the great cycle of figures with images of the emperor and the seven electors on the façade. The approximately life-sized figures are identified by coats of arms or imperial insignia. From the left, the series runs like this: the emperor, the ecclesiastical electors of Mainz, Trier and Cologne, and the secular rulers of Bohemia, Rhineland-Palatinate, Saxony and Brandenburg. The Bremen council paid tribute to the emperor, not the local ruler, thus aligning itself with the electors and showing the self-confidence of an imperial city even then. Other figures on the narrow sides are the city's patron saint, Peter – facing the cathedral – as well as Old Testament prophets exhorting justice. There is no further information available about the other medieval design elements on the façade, the coats of arms and tondi are lost.

The new façade design executed between 1608 and 1616 retained the cycle with the emperor and the electors, as the statement this made remained unchanged and valid. What was added now was a highly ambitious, elaborate and scholarly pictorial programme in the form of reliefs in places specially created for them. There are images of virtues, senses, arts, elements, seasons and other things, which makes the façade into an encyclopaedic overall image. 22 spandrels can be easily recognized from the market place. These list, in an additive series, the qualities and virtues distinguishing the council: philosophy, truth, watchfulness, care, work, diligence, generosity, strength, magnanimity, concord, patience, chastity, prudence, memory, faith, hope, solicitude, justice, moderation, wisdom, peace and fame. There are also pairs of figures in the friezes on the entablature areas of the projecting section, symbolizing the senses (sight, hearing, smell, taste, touch), the arts (grammar, dialectics, rhetoric, music, arithmetic, geometry, astronomy) and then the virtues again (love, faith, wisdom, hope, justice, peace, strength and moderation) and the elements (fire, water, earth and air). The façade programme is completed by the seasons, planets, evangelists ad the so-called battles of souls (psychomachia). The building itself is concluded with fully three-dimensional free figures in the roof zone, as corner acroteria and topping the gables of the dormers and the central projecting section. Here we have warriors, and the virtues yet again.

These depictions are there to glorify the governing council, a kind of panegyric self-representation of the kind that is frequently found in other buildings associated with rulers at this time. The city's freedom and the aims of public welfare and justice for this city are expressed in the architecture and in the pictorial programme.

The iconography continues in the interior as well. The large murals by Bartholomäus Bruyn dating from 1532 show the act of founding the city, with Charlemagne handing the cathedral over to Bishop Willehad, a reference to the city's imperial freedom and the Judgement of Solomon, to be understood as an exhortation to justice. The wood carvings in the Güldenkammer pursue the themes addressed on the exterior. Planets, deities and warriors adorn the parapet above the stairs. A fully sculpted figures of Hercules, alongside reliefs of the senses and virtues, decorates the newel post on the stairs, and a statue of Justice with warriors and the Bremen coat of arms borne by lions enhance the portal. Paintings depicting Justice are let into the walls of the Güldenkammer on the upper-hall side.

Direct and indirect models from a variety of engravings can be named in association with the images on the town hall, proving the high level of knowledge and zeal about education driving those responsible in their wishes for the town hall decoration and furnishings.

The Roland

Even though the monumental figure of Roland in the market place is detached from the town hall, it is inseparably associated with it. The figure was set up in the market place in 1414 as the first move in the project as a whole, possibly as a kind of herald of what was to change with the construction of the new town hall. It certainly expresses the new self-confidence found by the councillors, who were now acting as independent politicians. The legendary figure of Roland, who was part of Charlemagne's retinue, appears repeatedly as a general allegorical symbol of the cities' right to be free and to hold markets. About 40 Rolands are still in existence today, but the Bremen Roland stands out among the other survivors in many respects: it is the oldest, largest and artistically most important statue of this kind, and as it is almost free-standing – it has only a small support on its back, carrying the Gothic baldachin that protects it – it is also the one of the oldest free-standing figures north of the Alps. The particular austerity of the design and the height of the figure – over 5 m – make it stand out. Rolands very often stand for market rights, but the Bremen Roland makes a very concrete statement: the buckle on his belt is in the form of an angel playing a lute and this and the rose on his belt identify his as a martyr, and thus to be seen as the

ser stede ghegheuen ...« (Freiheit, die ich euch offenbare, die Karl ... dieser Stätte gegeben hat ...) Damit wird die bis heute anhaltende Unabhängigkeit der Stadt anschaulich begründet.

Das Neue Rathaus

Im 19. Jahrhundert nahmen die Aufgaben der Verwaltung der Städte stark zu. Nach der Reichsgründung 1871 wurden so in vielen großen Städten neue, umfangreiche Verwaltungsbauten an der Stelle der alten oder an neuen Standorten errichtet. Bremen, das durch enormen Zuwachs der Handelsaktivität in dieser Zeit reich und auf rund 150 000 Einwohner angewachsen war, hätte leicht einen großen Gesamtneubau errichten können. Stattdessen schrieb man 1903 einen ersten und 1907 einen zweiten Architekturwettbewerb aus, um die geeigneten Formen für eine vorsichtige rückwärtige Erweiterung zu finden. 1909–13 wurde der Bau nach Plänen des Münchener Architekten Gabriel von Seidl ausgeführt. Das Raumprogramm wurde auf die Funktionen der Regierungskanzlei reduziert, andere sonst in modernen Rathäusern versammelte Aufgaben wurden ausgelagert. Nur so war es möglich, dieses Projekt auf den zur Verfügung stehenden Flächen umzusetzen, ohne das Alte Rathaus anzutasten. In einfühlsamer Art wurde durch die Überwindung historischer Gestaltungsprinzipien ein sich unterordnender Bau entwickelt, der sich neben den vorsichtig aus der Renaissance abgeleiteten Details auch im Material (Klinker, Naturstein, Kupfer) anpasst.

Mit dem Erweiterungsbau wurde das Alte Rathaus entlastet, und es blieben ihm allein die herausgehobenen repräsentativen Funktionen vorbehalten. Allein der Ratskeller wird unverändert bis heute für Weinlagerung, Verkauf und Gastronomie genutzt. Ratssitzungen, die früher in der Oberen Halle stattfanden, Kanzleinutzung und Aktenarchivierung verlagerte man in den Erweiterungsbau. Dieser erhielt dafür eine Raumfolge, die sich um einen kleinen Innenhof herum gruppiert und an die Obere Halle im Alten Rathauses anschließt. Für weniger bedeutsame festliche Anlässe wurde im Neuen Rathaus ein weiterer Festsaal eingerichtet. Im Westtrakt sind nun hierarchisch geordnet in Rang und Größe die repräsentativen Räume aufgereiht: Obere Halle (Altes Rathaus), Festsaal, Kaminzimmer, Gobelinzimmer (Neues Rathaus). Am Gelenkpunkt zwischen Nord- und Ostflügel findet der Senatssaal seinen Platz, daneben reihen sich auf der Hauptetage weitere Büroräume, wobei zum Dom hin als Endpunkt das Zimmer des Bürgermeisters liegt.

Der Komplex des Erweiterungsbaus wird über ein neues Portal auf der Südostseite betreten, über dem die Inschrift »SPQB« (Senatus Populusque Bremensis – Senat und Volk von Bremen) den Geist der freien Stadtrepublik auch in der deutschen Kaiserzeit nach außen kennzeichnet.

Zwei großzügige Treppenanlagen und weiträumige Wandelhallen mit wertvollen Ausstattungen erschließen den Erweiterungsbau. Dabei ergibt sich die Möglichkeit, Festgesellschaften, wie die Schaffermahlzeit, das älteste seit 1545 bestehende Brudermahl, durch die Untere Halle und über eine repräsentative Freitreppe in die Obere Halle zu geleiten. Ohne übertriebenen Prunk und an vielen Stellen mit qualitätvollen Details wird auf die lange Tradition der Freien Hansestadt Bremen Bezug genommen.

Das Rathaus heute

Das Rathaus ist bis heute unverändert Sitz der Regierung des Bundeslandes Bremen. Der Präsident des Senats, der Bürgermeister, ist zusammen mit der Verwaltung seiner Senatskanzlei im Gebäude untergebracht. Die Sitzungen des Senats, des Regierungskabinetts, finden traditionell im Senatssaal statt. Auch andere repräsentative staatliche Veranstaltungen werden in den Räumen des Alten und Neuen Rathauses durchgeführt. Damit dient dieser Bau den gleichen Aufgaben, für die er vor über 600 Jahren errichtet wurde: der Staatsrepräsentation der Freien Hansestadt Bremen.

Mit der Aufnahme in die Liste des Weltkulturerbes der UNESCO im Jahr 2004 ist nicht nur die herausragende architekturhistorische und kulturelle Bedeutung des Rathauses ausgezeichnet worden, sondern man ist damit auch die besondere Verpflichtung eingegangen, das Rathaus und den Roland auf höchstem Niveau zu pflegen. Strenge denkmalpflegerische Ansprüche gelten nicht nur für den Bau selbst, sondern auch für sein Umfeld, die sogenannte Pufferzone.

Das Rathaus ist seit Jahrhunderten stets mit besonderem Respekt behandelt und instand gehalten worden. Kontinuierliche Pflege war immer oberste Maxime. Traditionsbewusst hat man nur wenige und sorgsam geplante Modernisierungs- oder Anpassungsmaßnahmen durchgeführt. Im Falle von Schäden wird zurückhaltend repariert statt gänzlich erneuert. Ab 2001 fand eine mehrjährige, sorgfältig geplante Sanierung des Rathauses statt, die unter strenger Überwachung des Landesamts für Denkmalpflege stand. Dabei wurden mit historischen Materialien und alten Techniken Altersschäden behandelt. Historische Patina und unschädliche Altersspuren wurden dabei bewusst belassen. Um sicherzustellen, dass man auftretende Schäden frühzeitig erkennt und zeitnah behandeln kann, um damit größeren Substanzverlust zu vermeiden, unterliegt das Bremer Rathaus einer regelmäßigen Kontrolle und eines speziellen Objekt-Monitorings. So wird man den Anforderungen der UNESCO in besonderem Maße gerecht und kann gewährleisten, dass das Rathaus auch zukünftigen Generationen authentisch und original überliefert wird.

Literaturauswahl

Adamietz, Horsl, und Hans Münch, *Das Bremer Rathaus*, Bremen 1980.

Albrecht, Stephan, *Das Bremer Rathaus im Zeichen städtischer Selbstdarstellung vor dem 30jährigen Krieg*, Marburg 1993 (*Materialien zur Kunst- und Kulturgeschichte in Nord- und Westdeutschland*).

Albrecht, Stephan, *Mittelalterliche Rathäuser in Deutschland. Architektur und Funktion*, Darmstadt 2004.

Bader, Karl S., und Gerhard Dilcher, *Deutsche Rechtsgeschichte. Land und Stadt, Bürger und Bauer im Alten Europa*, Berlin 1999.

Bippen, Wilhelm von, *Geschichte der Stadt Bremen*, 3 Bde, Bremen 1892–98.

Elmshäuser, Konrad, *Geschichte Bremens*, München 2007.

Elmshäuser, Konrad, Hans-Christoph Hoffmann und Hans-Joachim Manske (Hrsg.), *Welterbeantrag. Das Rathaus und der Roland auf dem Marktplatz in Bremen*, Bremen (2001) 2003.

Goerlitz, Theodor, *Der Ursprung und die Bedeutung der Rolandsbilder*, Weimar 1934.

Gramatzki, Rolf, *Das Rathaus in Bremen. Versuch zu seiner Ikonologie*, Bremen 1994.

Gruber, Karl, *Das deutsche Rathaus*, München 1943.

Hägermann, Dieter, »Das Barbarossa-Diplom und seine Bedeutung für die Entwicklung der Stadt Bremen«, in: *Bremisches Jahrbuch*, Bd. 65, Bremen 1987.

Hägermann, Dieter, »Bremens Weg zur Freien Reichsstadt«, in: *Bremisches Jahrbuch*, Bd. 76, Bremen 1997.

Manske, Hans-Joachim (Hrsg.), *The Town Hall and Roland on the Market Place of Bremen. Their Special Significance in Comparison to Other Town Halls*, Bremen 2003.

Müller, Hartmut:, »Das Linzer Diplom von 1646«, in: *Bremisches Jahrbuch*, Bd. 74/75, Bremen 1995/96.

Paul, Jürgen, *Die mittelalterlichen Kommunalpaläste in Italien*, Köln 1965.

Paul, Jürgen, »Das Rathaus im Kaiserreich. Kunstpolitische Aspekte einer Bauaufgabe des 19. Jahrhunderts«, in: *Kunst, Kultur und Politik im deutschen Kaiserreich*, Bd. 4, Berlin 1982.

Rempel, Hans, *Die Rolandstatuen*, Darmstadt 1989.

Schwarzwälder, Herbert, *Die Geschichte der Freien Hansestadt Bremen*, 5 Bde, Bremen 1975–85.

Skalecki, Georg, »Das Rathaus und der Roland auf dem Marktplatz in Bremen als Weltkulturerbe der UNESCO«, in: *Denkmalpflege in Bremen*, 2, Bremen 2005, S. 8 bis 29.

Skalecki, Georg, *Deutsche Architektur zur Zeit des Dreißigjährigen Krieges. Der Einfluß Italiens auf das deutsche Bauschaffen*, Regensburg 1989.

Stein, Rudolf, *Romanische, gotische und Renaissancebaukunst in Bremen*, Bremen 1962.

Selected bibliography

Adamietz, Horst, and Hans Münch, *Das Bremer Rathaus*, Bremen, 1980.

Albrecht, Stephan, *Das Bremer Rathaus im Zeichen städtischer Selbstdarstellung vor dem 30jährigen Krieg*, Marburg, 1993 (*Materialien zur Kunst- und Kulturgeschichte in Nord- und Westdeutschland*).

Albrecht, Stephan, *Mittelalterliche Rathäuser in Deutschland. Architektur und Funktion*, Darmstadt, 2004.

Bader, Karl S., and Gerhard Dilcher, *Deutsche Rechtsgeschichte. Land und Stadt, Bürger und Bauer im Alten Europa*, Berlin, 1999.

Bippen, Wilhelm von, *Geschichte der Stadt Bremen*, 3 vols, Bremen, 1892–98.

Elmshäuser, Konrad, *Geschichte Bremens*, Munich, 2007.

Elmshäuser, Konrad, Hans-Christoph Hoffmann and Hans-Joachim Manske (eds), *Welterbeantrag. Das Rathaus und der Roland auf dem Marktplatz in Bremen*, Bremen (2001), 2003.

Goerlitz, Theodor, *Der Ursprung und die Bedeutung der Rolandsbilder*, Weimar, 1934.

Gramatzki, Rolf, *Das Rathaus in Bremen. Versuch zu seiner Ikonologie*, Bremen, 1994.

Gruber, Karl, *Das deutsche Rathaus*, Munich, 1943.

Hägermann, Dieter, »Das Barbarossa-Diplom und seine Bedeutung für die Entwicklung der Stadt Bremen«, in: *Bremisches Jahrbuch*, vol. 65, Bremen, 1987.

Hägermann, Dieter, »Bremens Weg zur Freien Reichsstadt«, in: *Bremisches Jahrbuch*, vol. 76, Bremen, 1997.

Manske, Hans-Joachim (ed.), *The Town Hall and Roland on the Market Place of Bremen. Their Special Significance in Comparison to Other Town Halls*, Bremen, 2003.

Müller, Hartmut:, »Das Linzer Diplom von 1646«, in: *Bremisches Jahrbuch*, vol. 74/75, Bremen, 1995/96.

Paul, Jürgen, *Die mittelalterlichen Kommunalpaläste in Italien*, Cologne, 1965.

Paul, Jürgen, »Das Rathaus im Kaiserreich. Kunstpolitische Aspekte einer Bauaufgabe des 19. Jahrhunderts«, in: *Kunst, Kultur und Politik im deutschen Kaiserreich*, vol. 4, Berlin, 1982.

Rempel, Hans, *Die Rolandstatuen*, Darmstadt, 1989.

Schwarzwälder, Herbert, *Die Geschichte der Freien Hansestadt Bremen*, 5 vols, Bremen, 1975–85.

Skalecki, Georg, »Das Rathaus und der Roland auf dem Marktplatz in Bremen als Weltkulturerbe der UNESCO«, in: *Denkmalpflege in Bremen*, 2, Bremen, 2005, pp. 8 to 29.

Skalecki, Georg, *Deutsche Architektur zur Zeit des Dreißigjährigen Krieges. Der Einfluß Italiens auf das deutsche Bauschaffen*, Regensburg, 1989.

Stein, Rudolf, *Romanische, gotische und Renaissancebaukunst in Bremen*, Bremen, 1962.

concrete historic Roland, Margrave of Brittany, who travelled in the Emperor's retinue. So he is the real messenger of Charlemagne, who is here conferring imperial freedom on Bremen as a special right for the city. The shield – the present one dates from 1512 – explains this even more concretely: »vryheit do ik ju openbar de karl ... desser stede ghegheuen ...« (freedom that I reveal to you, that Charles ... has given this place ...) This is a vivid demonstration of the city's independence, which continues today.

The new town hall

In the 19th century, city administrations had a very great deal more to do. So after the foundation of the Second German Empire in 1871, many big cities built new and extensive administrative buildings to replace old one, or on new sites. Bremen saw a huge increase in trading activity at this time, making the city rich and increasing the population to about 150,000 inhabitants, so it could easily have opted for a large and completely new building. Instead of this, architectural competitions were announced in 1903 and 1907 to find a suitable approach for careful extension at the back. The building went up from 1909 to 1913, designed by the Munich architect Gabriel von Seidl. The spatial programme was confined to facilities for the government offices, and other functions that are sometimes brought together in modern town halls were moved out. This was the only way in which it was possible to implement this project in the space available, without touching the old town hall. Historical design principles were sensitively set aside to produce a self-effacing building that conformed in terms of materials (clinker, natural stone, copper), as well as using details carefully derived from the Renaissance.

The new building took the pressure off the old town hall; all it now had to do was to carry out the most prestigious and lofty functions. Only the Ratskeller remains unchanged until today, and is still used for storing wine, sales and catering. Council meetings, which used to take place in the upper hall, office functions and the filing of records and documents were shifted to the new building. This was given a sequence of rooms for this purpose grouped around a little inner courtyard and adjacent to the upper hall of the old town hall. Another banqueting hall was included in the new town hall for less important events and celebrations. The rooms intended for representation are now arranged in rank and size in the western section: upper hall (old town hall), banqueting hall, fireplace room, gobelin room (new town hall). The senate hall is placed at the hinge point between the east and the north wing. Next to this are further offices on the main floor, with the mayor's office as the end point at the cathedral end.

A new portal gives access to the extension. The inscription »SPQB« above this (Senatus Populusque Bremensis – the Senate and People of Bremen) proclaims the spirit of the free city republic at the time of the German empire as well.

Two lavish staircases and spacious foyers with choice decoration and furnishings give access to the extension. This makes it possible to condict groups who are celebrating, like the Schaffermahlzeit, the oldest fraternal feast, in existence since 1545, through the lower hall and into the upper hall via an imposing open-air staircase. The long tradition of the Free Hanseatic City of Bremen is cited without undue pomp and in many places with high-quality detailing.

The town hall today

The town hall remains as it has always been, the seat of government for the Federal *Land* of Bremen. The president of the senate, the mayor, is accommodated in the building, along with his senate offices. Meetings of the senate, the governing cabinet, traditionally take place in the senate hall. Other prestigious state events are held in the rooms of the old and new town halls. Thus the building is doing the same job it was built to do over 600 years ago: state representation for the Free Hanseatic City of Bremen.

Inclusion on UNESCO's World Heritage List in 2004 did not just identify the town hall's outstanding significance in terms of architectural history and culture, but also brought with it the particular duty of caring for the town hall and the Roland at the highest possible level. Strict monument conservation requirements apply both to the building itself and also for the area around it, the so-called buffer zone.

The town hall has always been treated and maintained with special respect for centuries. Continuous care was always the supreme watchword. Fully aware of tradition, its guardians have carried out only a very few carefully planned modernization and adaptation measures. If there is damage, it is carefully repaired rather than completely renewed. The town hall was refurbished over several years on the basis of a careful plan from 2001, and this was strictly supervised by the local monument conservation office. Damage caused by the age of the building was treated using historical materials and old techniques. Historic patina and innocuous traces of age were deliberately left. To ensure that any damage is recognized in good time and treated as soon as possible, to avoid greater loss of building substance, Bremen town hall is subject to regular checks and special building monitoring. This does justice to UNESCO's requirements in a special way, and can guarantee that the town hall will be passed down to future generations authentically and in its original form.

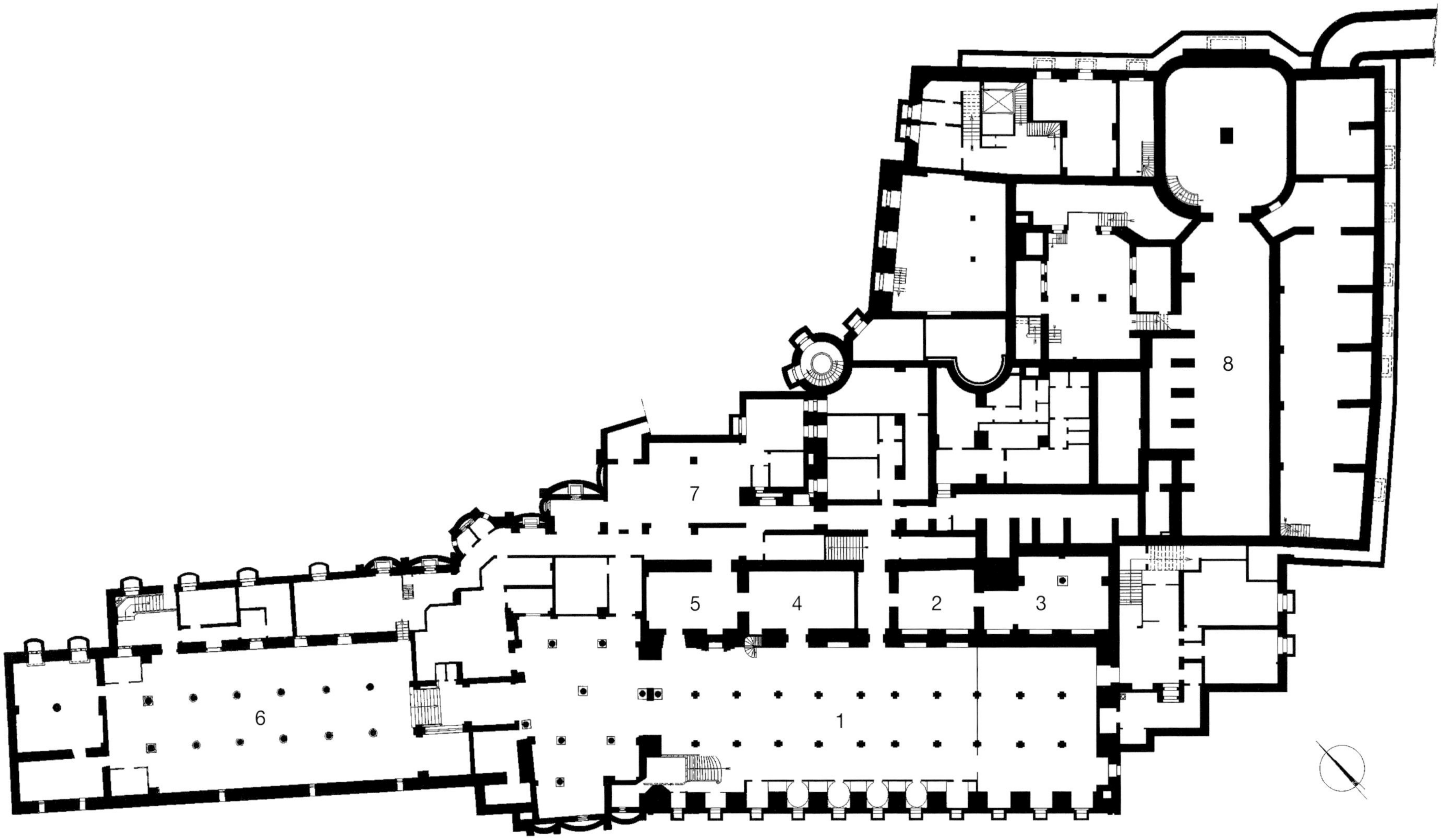

6. Marktplatz, Rathaus, Dom und Börsengebäude im Jahr 1888. (Landesamt für Denkmalpflege Bremen.)
7–9. Grundrisse (Kellergeschoss, Erdgeschoss, Hauptgeschoss). Legende: 1 Hauptkeller, 2 Apostelkeller, 3 Rosekeller, 4 Kaiserzimmer, 5 Senatszimmer, 6 Bacchuskeller, 7 Wirtschaftskeller, 8 Flaschenweinlager, 9 Untere Halle im Alten Rathaus, 10 Festtreppe, 11 Eingang zum Neuen Rathaus, 12 untere Halle im Neuen Rathaus, 13 Kanzleitrakt, 14 Obere Halle im Alten Rathaus, 15 Güldenkammer, 16 Festsaal, 17 Kaminzimmer, 18 Gobelinzimmer, 19 Senatssaal, 20 obere Halle im Neuen Rathaus, 21 Hansezimmer.

6. Market place, town hall, cathedral and stock exchange in 1888. (Landesamt für Denkmalpflege Bremen.)
7–9. Floor plans (basement, ground floor, main floor). Key: 1 main cellar, 2 Apostelkeller, 3 Rosekeller, 4 Kaiserzimmer, 5 Senatszimmer, 6 Bacchuskeller, 7 storeroom, 8 storeroom for bottled wines, 9 lower hall in the old town hall, 10 gala stairs, 11 entrance to the new town hall, 12 lower hall in the new town hall, 13 administration wing, 14 upper hall in the old town hall, 15 Güldenkammer, 16 banqueting hall, 17 fireplace room, 18 gobelin room, 19 senate hall, 20 upper hall in the new town hall, 21 Hanse room.

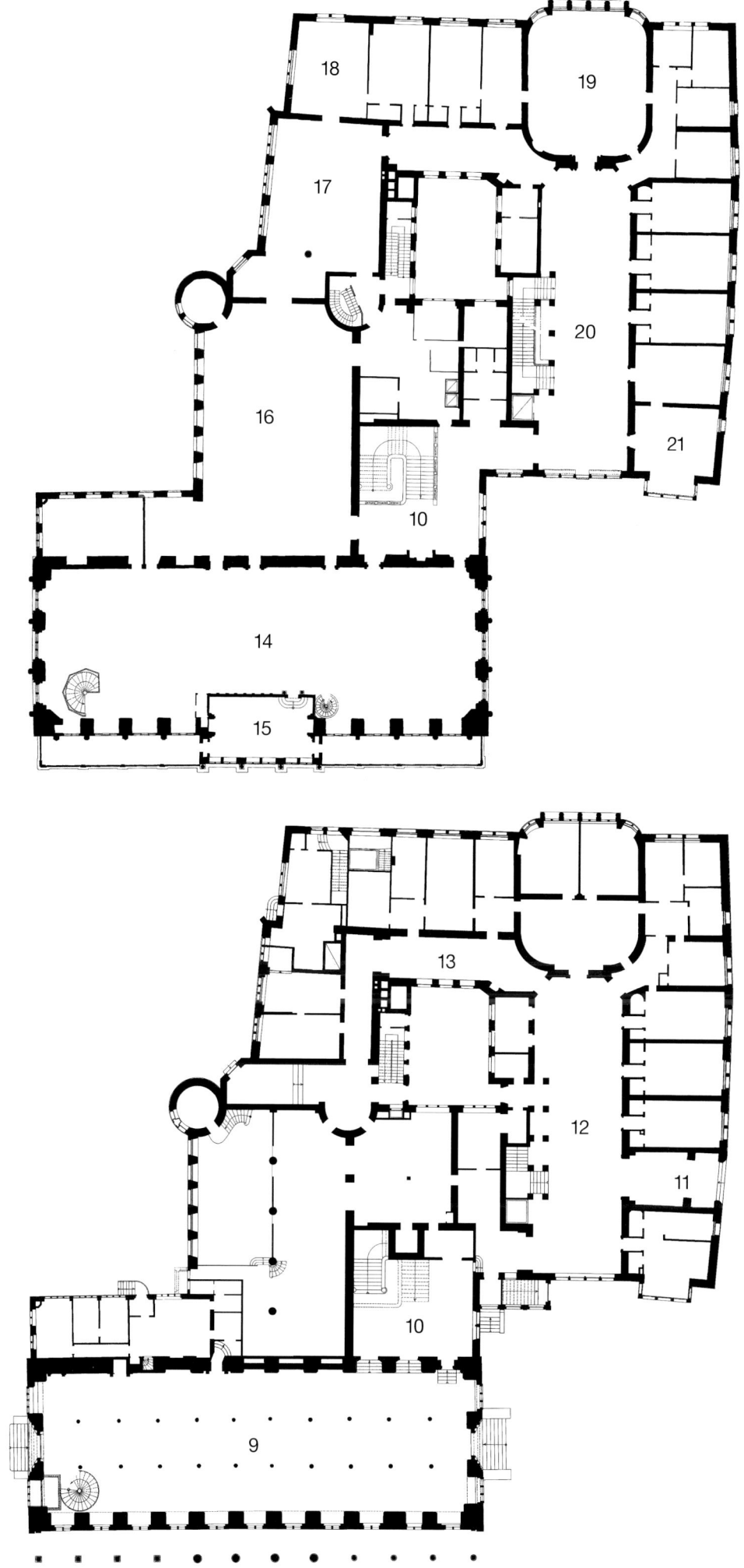

1. Gesamtansicht des Rathauses von Süden. Rechts der Dom; er liegt auf der höchsten Erhebung der Düne. Zu seinen Füßen entwickelte sich der Marktplatz.

1. General view of the town hall from the south. The cathedral on the right is situated on the highest point of the dune. The market place developed at its feet.

2. Ansicht des Alten Rathauses vom ehemaligen mittelalterlichen Schiffsanlegeplatz am Ufer der Balge, eines inzwischen zugeschütteten Arms der Weser. Rechts der Dom und das Haus der Bürgerschaft von Wassili Luckhardt.

2. View of the old town hall from the former medieval ship's mooring at the bank of the Balge, an arm of the Weser, which has been filled up in the meantime. On the right the cathedral and the Haus der Bürgerschaft (state parliament) by Wassili Luckhardt.

S. 28/29
3. Altes Rathaus, Südseite. Der Mittelrisalit tritt dominant in Erscheinung und verleiht dem ehemals gleichmäßigen rechteckigen gotischen Bau einen Kulminationspunkt.

p. 28/29
3. Old town hall, south side. The central projecting part dominates the building and adds a culminating point to the former regular rectangular Gothic building.

4. Altes Rathaus, Südseite, westlicher Fassadenbereich, Kaiser und geistliche Kurfürsten.
5. Altes Rathaus, Südseite, östlicher Fassadenbereich, weltliche Kurfürsten.

4. Old town hall, south side, detail of the western façade, emperor and clergy electors.
5. Old town hall, south side, detail of the eastern façade, secular electors.

6. Roland, 1404 als Auftakt der Neubaumaßnahme aufgestellt.
7. Roland, Detail mit Schild.

6. Roland, erected in 1404 to start the new construction of the town hall.
7. Roland, detail with shield.

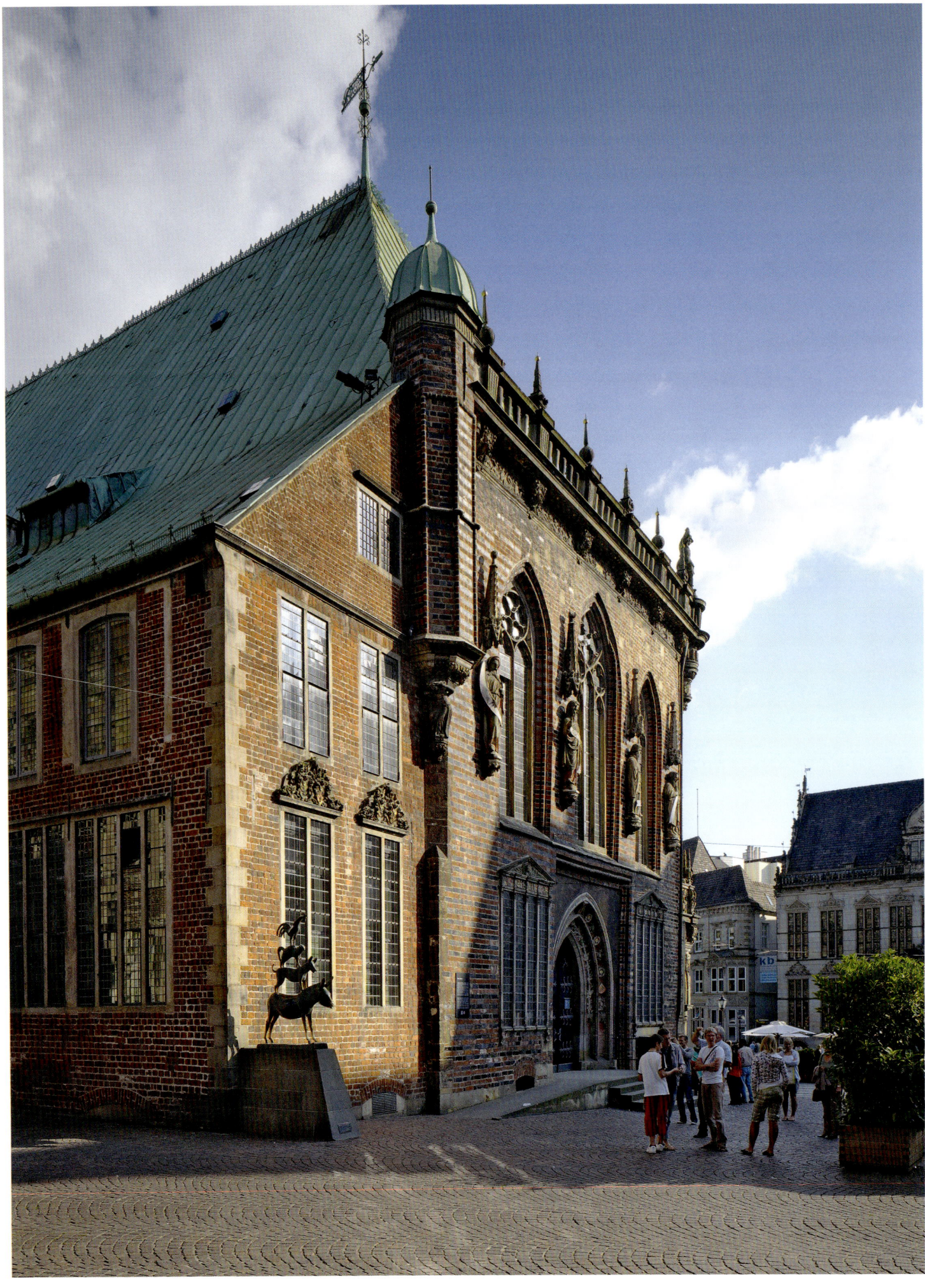

8. Altes Rathaus, Westseite, links die Gruppe der *Bremer Stadtmusikanten*, 1953 von Gerhard Marcks geschaffen.
9. Altes Rathaus, Westseite mit dem Zugang zum Ratskeller.
10. Neues Rathaus, Westseite.

8. Old town hall, west side, on the left the *Bremer Stadtmusikanten*, created in 1953 by Gerhard Marcks.
9. Old town hall, west side with the entrance to the Ratskeller.
10. New town hall, west side.

11. Neues Rathaus, Nordseite.
12. Neues Rathaus, Nordseite, Risalit des Senatssaals.

11. New town hall, north side.
12. New town hall, north, projecting part of the senate hall.

13. Neues Rathaus, Ostseite.
14. Neues Rathaus, Ostseite, Hauptportal mit der Inschrift »SPQB«.

13. New town hall, east side.
14. New town hall, east side, main portal with the inscription »SPQB«.

15. Altes Rathaus, Ostseite. Die Fenster des Obergeschosses stammen noch vom gotischen Gründungsbau. Links Petrus mit seinem Schlüssel, der zum Wappen der Stadt wurde.
16. Altes Rathaus, Ostseite. Den Zugang flankieren zwei Reiter (sog. Herolde), die von Rudolf Maison für die Pariser Weltausstellung 1900 geschaffen und vom Bankier Harjes seiner Heimatstadt Bremen gestiftet wurden.

15. Old town hall, east side. The windows of the upper floor are from the original Gothic building. On the left Peter with his key, which has become the arms of the town.
16. Old town hall, east side. The entrance is flanked by two riders (so called heralds), created by Rudolf Maison for the Paris 1900 world fair and donated to his home town Bremen by the banker Harjes.

17, 18. Altes Rathaus, Untere Halle, ehemals Kauf- und Markthalle sowie Ort des Niedergerichts. Dreischiffige Konstruktion mit Eichenholzständern.

17, 18. Old town hall, lower hall, former merchant and market hall as well as seat of the lower courts. Three aisles and oak uprights.

19. Altes Rathaus, Obere Halle. Die von der Decke hängenden Schiffsmodelle stammen aus dem 16., 17. und 18. Jahrhundert.

19. Old town hall, upper hall. The model ships are from the 16th, 17th, and 18th centuries.

20. Altes Rathaus, Obere Halle, Nordseite mit dem Walbild von Franz Wulfhagen von 1669. Den auf dem Bild dargestellten Wal rangen die Bremer den Schweden ab.
21. Altes Rathaus, Obere Halle, Portal mit einer Tafel von 1491, auf der Regeln für eine weise und gerechte Regierung niedergeschrieben sind.

20. Old town hall, upper hall, north side with the painting of a whale by Franz Wulfhagen from 1669. The whale shown on the painting was wrung from the Swedes by the people of Bremen.
21. Old town hall, upper hall, portal with a plate on which rules for a wise and fair government are written down.

22. Altes Rathaus, Obere Halle, Nordseite, Wandgemälde des »Salomonischen Urteils« von Bartolomäus Bruyn von 1532. Darunter befand sich das alte Ratsgestühl.

22. Old town hall, upper hall, north side, mural of the »Judgement of Solomon« by Bartolomäus Bruyn from 1532. Underneath were the old council's chairs.

23. Altes Rathaus, Obere Halle, Nordseite, Wandgemälde mit der Darstellung der Gründungsgeschichte von Bartolomäus Bruyn von 1532: Karl der Große übergibt Bischof Willehad den Dom.

23. Old town hall, upper hall, north side, mural showing the foundation story by Bartolomäus Bruyn from 1532: Charlemagne hands over the cathedral to Bishop Willehad.

S. 50/51
24. Altes Rathaus, Güldenkammer mit der Einrichtung von Heinrich Vogeler von 1905.

25. Neues Rathaus, Foyer im Erdgeschoss.
26. Neues Rathaus, Treppe zum Hauptgeschoss.

p. 50/51
24. Old town hall, Güldenkammer, furnished by Heinrich Vogeler in 1905.

25. New town hall, foyer on the ground floor.
26. New town hall, stairs leading to the main floor.

27, 28. Neues Rathaus, Raum mit der Festtreppe zwischen Erd- und Hauptgeschoss.
29. Neues Rathaus, obere Halle, am Ende der Senatssaal.

27, 28. New town hall, space with the gala stairs between ground floor and main floor.
29. New town hall, upper hall, at the end the senate hall.

30, 31. Neues Rathaus, Blick von der oberen Halle in den Raum mit der Festtreppe.
32. Neues Rathaus, nördliches Ende der oberen Halle, in der Mitte der Zugang zum Senatssaal.

30, 31. New town hall, view of the space with the gala stairs from the upper hall.
32. New town hall, northern end of the upper hall, in the centre the entrance to the senate hall.

S. 58/59
33. Neues Rathaus, Senatssaal.

p. 58/59
33. New town hall, senate hall.

p. 60/61

34. New town hall, banqueting hall with ladies' gallery and gallery for musicians.

35. New town hall, banqueting hall, painting of the Weser front by Carl Vinnen.

36. New town hall, tower room as »Kaiserkabinett« with bronze relief of Kaiser Wilhelm III by Adolf von Hildebrand.

37. Neues Rathaus, Kaminzimmer.
38. Neues Rathaus, Blick vom Kaminzimmer in den Gang zur oberen Halle.

37. New town hall, fireplace room.
38. Neues Rathaus, view from the fireplace room into the corridor leading to the upper hall.

39, 40. Neues Rathaus, Gobelinzimmer mit einem französischen Gobelin aus der 1. Hälfte des 17. Jahrhunderts mit einem Artemis-Zyklus.
41. Neues Rathaus, Bibliothekszimmer, gestaltet von dem bekannten Schriftsteller, Architekten und Innenraumgestalter Rudolf Alexander Schröder. Diese Raumausstattung stammt aus der Villa des Kaufmanns und Kunstmäzens Leopold Biermann.

39, 40. New town hall, gobelin room with a French gobelin from the first half of the 17th century with an Artemis series.
41. Neues Rathaus, library room, designed by the well-known writer, architect and interior designer Rudolf Alexander Schröder. This interior decoration comes from the villa of the businessman and art patron Leopold Biermann.

42. Altes Rathaus, Kellergeschoss, Hauptraum mit Weinfässern des 17. und 18. Jahrhunderts, deren Böden schmuckvoll dekoriert sind.
43. Altes Rathaus, Kellergeschoss, Hauffkeller mit Fresken von Max Slevogt, die dieser nach den *Phantasien im Bremer Ratskeller* von Wilhelm Hauff 1927 malte.
44. Altes Rathaus, Kellergeschoss, Bacchuskeller, heute mit dem Ratskeller verbunden, ehemals Keller des Börsengebäudes von 1620, das westlich vor dem Rathaus stand.

42. Old town hall, basement, main room with wine casks of the 17th and 18th centuries with highly decorated bottoms.
43. Old town hall, basement, Hauffkeller with frecoes by Max Slevogt, who painted them in 1927 after the *Phantasien im Bremer Ratskeller* by Wilhelm Hauff.
44. Old town hall, basement, Bacchuskeller, today connected with the Ratskeller, formerly cellar of the stock exchange from 1620, which was situated west of the town hall.

45. Altes Rathaus, Kellergeschoss, Blick vom Kaiserzimmer in das Senatszimmer, beide 1875 vom Historienmaler Arthur Fitger ausgemalt.
46. Altes Rathaus, Kellergeschoss, Rosekeller mit Fassweinen von 1653.

45. Old town hall, basement, view of the Senatszimmer from the Kaiserzimmer, both decorated in 1875 by the historical painter Arthur Fitger.
46. Old town hall, basement, Rosekeller with cask wines from 1653.

Dank allen, die zur Entstehtung dieses Buches beigetragen haben, besonders dem Senator für Kultur der Freien Hansestadt Bremen und der Bremen Marketing Gesellschaft.

Thanks to everyone who has helped to bring this book into being, especially the culture senator for the Free Hanseatic City of Bremen and the Bremen Marketing Gesellschaft.